The Informational Writing Toolkit

Using Mentor Texts in Grades 3–5

Sean Ruday

Routledge
Taylor & Francis Group

NEW YORK AND LONDON

First published 2015
by Routledge
711 Third Avenue, New York, NY 10017

and by Routledge
2 Park Square, Milton Park, Abingdon, Oxon OX14 4RN

Routledge is an imprint of the Taylor & Francis Group, an informa business

Library of Congress Cataloging-in-Publication Data
Ruday, Sean. The informational writing toolkit : Using mentor texts in
   grades 3–5 / Sean Ruday.
      pages cm
   Includes bibliographical references.
  1. English language—Study and teaching (Elementary)   2. Report
writing—Study and teaching (Elementary)   I. Title.
   LB1576.R777 2015
   372.62'3—dc23
   2014027607

ISBN: 978-1-138-83204-6 (hbk)
ISBN: 978-1-138-83206-0 (pbk)
ISBN: 978-1-315-73623-5 (ebk)

Typeset in Palatino and Formata
by Apex Covantage, LLC

Contents

Meet the Author

Sean Ruday is an assistant professor of English Education at Longwood University. He began his teaching career at a public school in Brooklyn, New York, and has taught English and language arts in New York, Massachusetts, and Virginia. He holds a BA from Boston College, an MA from New York University, and a PhD from the University of Virginia. Some publications in which his articles have appeared are *Journal of Teaching Writing*, *Journal of Language and Literacy Education*, *Contemporary Issues in Technology and Teacher Education*, and the *Yearbook of the Literacy Research Association*. Sean is a frequent presenter at regional and national conferences. He enjoys talking with teachers about innovative ways to improve students' literacy learning. You can follow him on Twitter @SeanRuday and his professional website is seanruday.weebly.com. This is his third book with Routledge Eye on Education.

Acknowledgments

I am thankful for all of the support and assistance I have received while writing this book. I greatly appreciate the teachers who opened their classrooms to me, allowing me to work with their students. Similarly, I am grateful for the wonderful students in those classes who eagerly dove into the ideas and tools of informational writing. I would also like to thank the students whose writings are included in this book; I am thrilled to feature their works. I am very thankful for the guidance and support of this book's editor, Lauren Davis, who has been a wonderfully encouraging presence in my writing career. I would like to thank my parents, Bob and Joyce Ruday, for all that they have done for me. I am beyond grateful for their love and support. I also want to thank my wife, Clare Ruday, who brightens my life by bringing humor and happiness to it.

eResources

Many of the tools in this book can be downloaded and printed for class-room use. You can access these downloads by visiting the book product page on our website: www.routledge.com/books/details/9781138832060. Then click on the tab that says "eResources," and select the files. They will begin downloading to your computer.

"The Tools of Informational Writing": Helping Students Understand the Relationship between Mentor Texts and Their Own Informational Writing

I was recently conducting a professional development session on writing instruction and the Common Core Standards when a third-grade teacher named Amanda shared an important concern: "I'm stressed out about the Common Core's requirement that students write more informational texts. I think I'm good at teaching my students to write fictional and personal narratives, but not informational texts. I'm not sure about the best way to teach students to write them." Heads nodded around the room in response to Amanda's comment. Other teachers echoed her sentiments, explaining that this was the element of the Common Core Writing Standards that concerned them the most.

In response to these important observations, I asked the teachers what kinds of texts were most prevalent in their classrooms.

"Definitely fiction," one replied.

"Yes, a lot of fiction texts," responded another. "Different kinds of fictional genres—fantasy, historical, realistic."

Another teacher stated, "A bunch of fictional series. For example, my fourth graders are really into the books in the Lunch Lady series right now."

"This is great to know," I replied, "and I'm really excited about helping you teach your students to write informational texts. The first step is to show your students some really good informational texts written by published authors. Once your students have seen these published informational texts, you can talk with them about what makes these pieces effective. After that, the students can write their own informational pieces, using strategies the published authors utilized in their works."

"So, we're going to use informational writings as mentor texts?" asked a teacher.

"Exactly!" I exclaimed. "I was about to say that, and you beat me to it! Students need to see mentor texts of whatever we're asking them to write. In order to make our students effective *writers* of informational texts, we need to first help them become strong *readers* of informational texts. Once our students have read informational texts, we can talk with them about what the authors of those informational texts do. When students understand what these published authors do, they can apply these same ideas to their own works."

"That sounds wonderful," responded Amanda, the teacher whose comment began this conversation. "I feel a lot better about teaching my students to write informational texts now." I smiled, excited about helping these teachers use informational mentor texts in their classes.

This account of my conversation with these elementary school teachers is meant to provide an introduction to the ideas and instructional methods described in this book. I decided to write this book to provide a resource to elementary school teachers who are looking for additional support as they seek to help their students write informational texts. As you'll notice from the research cited in this book, informational writing instruction is both a challenge and a very important educational concept. This book presents research-based and classroom-tested ideas designed to help elementary school teachers use mentor texts to deepen their students' understandings of informational writing and ultimately help their students apply the strategies used by published authors to their own informational works.

This introductory chapter is divided into the following sections, each of which addresses a key element of this book's approach:

◆ The importance of informational writing
◆ The significance of mentor texts
◆ The toolkit metaphor
◆ The gradual release of responsibility
◆ What to expect in this book, including the specific Common Core Writing Standards this book addresses

The Importance of Informational Writing

As Amanda and the other teachers described in the opening section communicated, teaching informational writing is often associated with the Common Core State Standards. The CCSS emphasize the importance of reading and writing informational text, calling for students to be familiar with "biographies and autobiographies; books about history, social studies, science, and the arts; technical texts, including directions, forms, and information displayed in graphs, charts, or maps; and digital sources on a range of topics" (Common Core State Standards, 2010). The Common Core State Standards also identify informational writing as crucial to college and career readiness, explaining that college and career-ready students develop strong content knowledge; write with an awareness of audience, task, purpose, and discipline; and use relevant evidence—all features of strong informational writing. This focus on informational text represents an instructional shift in many elementary classrooms, where informational texts have traditionally been de-emphasized (Duke, 2000) and writing instruction has frequently focused on students composing creative works instead of informational ones (Newkirk, 1989).

In addition to the fact that informational writing is emphasized in the Common Core State Standards, there are a number of research-based reasons why focusing on informational writing in our elementary school classrooms is a great idea. Doing so can motivate our students, provide them with authentic writing experiences, and prepare them for the kinds of writing they'll do later in life. In this section, we'll explore those three reasons—motivation, authenticity, and preparation—in greater detail, examining seminal research on these topics. The studies cited here are especially important works that support the use of informational writing in the elementary classroom. In fact, some of these studies date back to the 1980s—showing that, while the Common Core Standards may be new, researchers have known for a long time that informational writing is an important topic to address with our elementary school writers!

Motivation

The use of informational writing in the elementary classroom provides students with increased opportunities to explore topics of interest to them. Since students who write informational text are frequently given opportunities to be experts on topics that are important to them and their peers, informational writing comes with a built-in motivational force. Students who research high-interest topics, write about them, and share their works with others are much more motivated to learn than those who do not have these opportunities (Guthrie & Alao, 1987). This is especially true with struggling students: students who have difficulty reading and writing are often more motivated and successful when given the chance to read and write informational text (Caswell & Duke, 1998). In this book, we'll examine specific situations where informational writing motivated otherwise reluctant and struggling students to fully engage in literacy. For example, we'll look closely at a fourth grader who explains how researching and writing about the animals in his community motivated him in ways that his previous language arts classes did not.

Authenticity

Informational writing can be motivating to students because of its authenticity: students who write informational texts frequently have a number of authentic, or real-world, audiences for their works. For example, students can share their informational writings by creating community newsletters about important local events, issues, and environmental developments. I recently worked with a fifth-grade class that created an informational pamphlet focused on the major festivals in its community. The students researched the history of these festivals, interviewed community members, and ultimately produced a resource that was widely shared in their town. This is an example of a situation in which students' works are written for a wider audience than just their teachers; students' informational writings can be contributions to ongoing conversations about real-world situations and may be read by a number of readers. In this book, we'll encounter students who have never before written for audiences other than their teacher and observe the different authentic ways they share their works.

Preparation

Another important attribute of informational writing is it prepares students for the kinds of work they will do as they get older. While many elementary school students write primarily fictional and personal narratives, older students and adults write a great deal of informational text (Newkirk, 1989). Since research also reveals that elementary school students *can* understand the features and structures of informational texts (Newkirk, 1989), there is no reason not to integrate these texts into our elementary classrooms. In this book, we'll examine specific methods to help our elementary school students write informational texts; these methods align with the Common Core Standards and will prepare our students for the kinds of writing they'll continue do in the future.

The Significance of Mentor Texts

In order for our elementary school students to be able to write their own informational texts, we teachers must first show them examples of high-quality informational texts from which they can learn. These examples, called mentor texts, provide students with clear models of what effective informational writing looks like and facilitate conversations about what strategies published authors use when crafting their works. Once students understand the strategies used by published writers, they can apply those same ideas to their own writings.

Mentor texts are used in all genres of writing instruction. Katie Wood Ray, in her book *Wondrous Words* (1999), explains, "I am looking for texts that have something in them or about them that can add to my students' knowledge base of how to write well" (p. 188). Showing our students especially effective informational texts can add to the knowledge base that Ray describes. For example, if we want our students to compose strong conclusions in their informational writings, we should show them examples of effective conclusions in published informational texts. When recently working with a fifth-grade class on writing effective conclusions, I showed them a number of published examples, including the following conclusion of the "Attila the Hun" section in Joy Masoff's book, *Oh, Yikes: History's Grossest, Wackiest Moments* (2006): "Without Attila, the Hunnish empire soon crumbled. But new cities had been created because of him—and the continent of Europe—sliced up by a short, eye-rolling ruler with a rusty sword—would never be the same" (p. 4).

After showing them this example, I asked the fifth graders what struck them about this conclusion. One young man immediately raised his hand, saying, "It's funny, but it still makes a good point."

"A strong insight," I responded. "What point does it make?"

"That Attila the Hun was really important."

"Yeah," interjected another student. "The conclusion says that new cities were created because of Attila and Europe wouldn't be the same without him."

"Very nicely said, all of you," I replied. "Now, let's take this one step further: what can you learn from this example that you can use in the conclusions in your own informational writings?"

One student quickly answered, "I think it shows that our conclusions should say something about why the topic of the paper is important, but they can still be fun to read."

This excerpt illustrates one way that published informational texts can be used as examples of effective writing from which students can learn. In this situation, the students learned from Joy Masoff's conclusion about Attila the Hun that conclusions should highlight the importance of the paper's topic but can still contain the author's voice. When these students created their own conclusions to the informational texts they wrote, they looked to craft final sections similar to Masoff's: statements about their subjects' importance that included the author's individual style and personality.

The Toolkit Metaphor

When authors compose effective informational texts, they need to consider all of the important aspects of those texts, such as an introduction, a strong sense of organization, features that aid comprehension, key details that develop ideas, transition statements, specific vocabulary terms, and strong conclusions. I think of all of these aspects of effective informational text as "tools" of informational writing; each one is something authors use at a specific time and for a specific purpose.

When I talk with students about writing informational texts, I focus on the "writing toolkit" metaphor. I explain to them that writers of all levels learn a number of skills and strategies, which they then keep in their toolkits. For example, the Common Core Standards identify one important aspect of writing informational text as "Introducing a Topic" (Common Core State Standards, 2010). When students study published informational texts that contain strong introductions, discuss those examples, identify what makes them effective, and practice creating their own, they've added this writing strategy to their toolkits. A fourth-grade student once told me that he didn't believe he would ever be good at writing. I explained that his writing would improve as he developed more writing tools. "Once you've added more skills and strategies to your writing toolkit," I explained, "you'll know a bunch of ways to make your writing strong. When you know all of these ways to improve your writing and have all of these tools, writing will feel much easier and you'll have a lot more fun doing it."

The Gradual Release of Responsibility

The best writing instruction makes students active participants in the learning process (Fletcher & Portalupi, 2001). An especially effective way to ensure that young writers remain active and engaged while learning the tools of effective informational writing is through the gradual release of responsibility method of instruction, which has been shown to improve students' writing achievement levels (Fisher & Frey, 2003). In this method of instruction, students gradually take increased ownership of and responsibility for their learning. To put this instructional method into practice, teachers begin by introducing a particular concept to students, providing examples and explanations of it. At this initial point in the process, teachers take on the majority of the responsibility for the students' learning. Next, teachers work with their students on the concept by engaging them in interactive activities and answering questions the students have. At this stage, more of the learning responsibility is shared between the students and teachers. Finally, teachers ask students to work on the concept independently, checking in with them through one-on-one conferences while they do so. In this final stage, most of the learning responsibility is assumed by the students.

The gradual release of responsibility is integral to the writing instruction described in this book. You will notice that the instructional recommendations this book described embody this process; these recommendations will help you introduce informational writing strategies to your students, involve them in interactive activities that require them to take additional responsibility for their learning, and finally equip your students with the understandings and skills to apply these strategies to their own informational writings.

What to Expect in This Book

This book identifies the tools that the Common Core Standards say students need to be able to use in order to write effective informational texts and discusses specific, classroom-ready practices to help students acquire these tools. This book is divided into three sections:

◆ Section one, which focuses on informational writing strategies aligned with the Common Core Standards for grades three through five. Each of the seven sections in this chapter addresses an important element of informational writing and explains how to help your students grasp that concept. For consistency and ease of use, I've organized each chapter in this section in the following format:

- ◆ An introduction to the chapter's focal concept. This opening section provides a description and some examples of the focal concept addressed in the chapter.
- ◆ A discussion of why the concept is important to strong informational writing. This section explains why authors use this particular concept when writing informational text and includes mentor text examples to illustrate how the concept appears in published works.
- ◆ A classroom snapshot. Each snapshot contains a description of my experiences teaching the chapter's focal concept to a third-, fourth-, or fifth-grade class during my recent work at an elementary school. I've included these snapshots so you can see how I taught my students about these important aspects of informational writing and learn from these concrete examples as you work with your own students.
- ◆ Specific instructional recommendations. Each chapter closes with specific recommendations for you to keep in mind when engaging your students in learning activities that focus on these concepts.

◆ Section two, which focuses on "Putting it Together." One chapter in this section focuses on strategies to use when assessing your students' informational writings, while another chapter addresses final thoughts and tips that will help you as you put the ideas and recommendations described in this book into practice in your own classroom.

◆ Section three, which features the following resources designed to help you put this book's ideas into action. The resources included in this section are:

- ◆ The book's reference list.
- ◆ An annotated bibliography, which lists the examples of informational writing featured in this book, the aspect of effective informational writing featured in each example, and the Common Core Standard associated with that concept.
- ◆ An appendix, which contains easily reproducible graphic organizers and charts you can use when teaching your students about the aspects of informational writing described in this book.

The following table lists the aspects of informational writing described in this book, the chapters in which they are discussed, and the Common Core Writing Standards with which each aligns.

Aspect of Informational Writing	Chapter	Related Common Core Writing Standards
Introducing a topic	Chapter One	W.3.2a, W.4.2a, W.5.2a
Grouping related information together	Chapter Two	W.3.2a, W.4.2a, W.5.2a
Adding features that aid comprehension	Chapter Three	W.3.2a, W.4.2a, W.5.2a
Developing a topic	Chapter Four	W.3.2b, W.4.2b, W.5.2b
Linking ideas	Chapter Five	W.3.2c, W.4.2c, W.5.2c
Using precise language and domain-specific vocabulary	Chapter Six	W.4.2d, W.5.2d
Crafting a concluding section	Chapter Seven	W.3.2d, W.4.2e, W.5.2e

Teaching the strategies of informational writing to elementary school students can be a challenge, but this book will give you practical and useful information that you can use to help your students master this important genre. As you read this book, you'll understand the aspects of informational writing emphasized in the Common Core Standards, why they are important to effective writing, how published authors use them, and specific ways to put them into practice in your future classrooms. If you're ready to learn more about teaching informational writing, keep reading!

Section **1**

Informational Writing Strategies Aligned with the
Common Core Standards for Grades 3–5

1

Introducing a Topic

What Does "Introducing a Topic" Mean?

A fundamental step of effective informational writing is introducing the topic of a piece in a clear and engaging way. The Common Core Writing Standards highlight the importance of this concept, as Standards W.3.2a, W.4.2a, and W.5.2a emphasize the value of introducing a topic when writing informational text. In this chapter, we'll discuss the following: what "introducing a topic" means, why this concept is important for effective informational writing, a description of a lesson on this concept, and key recommendations for helping your students effectively introduce topics in their own informational writing.

Let's begin by examining what it means to introduce a topic. An introduction to a piece of informational writing is an opening section of one or more paragraphs that provides a brief "first look" at subject matter that will be further developed later in the text. For example, the informational book *Reptiles* by Melissa Stewart (2001) contains an introductory paragraph that shows the reader what the rest of the book will address in more detail: "A snake flicks its long tongue as it slithers along the ground. A turtle sits on a rotting log and basks in the sun. A crocodile grabs a fish with its mighty jaws. These are the images that come to mind when someone says the word 'reptile'" (p. 5).

Stewart's introduction provides enough information to illustrate to the reader that this book is about reptiles, but doesn't yet go into a great amount of detail. The "first look" provided by this introduction conveys the topic of this book, inviting readers to continue reading the text. In the next section of this chapter, we'll consider why creating an effective introduction is important to well-written informational texts.

Why Introducing a Topic is Important to Effective Informational Writing

Introducing a topic is important to effective informational writing because a well-crafted introduction should perform two key actions: 1) Engage the reader; and 2) introduce key content. A strong introduction to a piece of informational writing does more than begin a piece—it opens the work in a clear and purposeful way that shows the author's ability to capture the reader's attention while also conveying basic information about the book's topic. Figure 1.1 illustrates the two key actions introductions perform and why each one is important.

In this section, we'll discuss why these concepts are related to an effective introduction using some published works to illustrate how professional writers apply these principles to their own introductions. Let's begin by examining the opening section of Gary W. Davis' (1997) informational text *Coral Reef*: "The waters of the Caribbean Sea are warm and clear. On the surface, everything appears peaceful. But just below, rising from the bottom of the sea, there is a very busy place. It is the underwater community of the coral reef" (p. 4). In this introductory passage, Davis both engages the reader and introduces key content. Let's take a look at how he achieves each of these results.

First, we'll examine the way Davis grabs the reader's attention. The first two sentences of this introductory paragraph draw the reader in through descriptive language that allows the reader to visualize the Caribbean Sea. Without these sentences, we readers wouldn't be engaged with the text in such a clear and effective way. Davis' description of the "warm and clear" Caribbean Sea waters and his statement that "everything appears peaceful" appeal to the reader's senses and allow a reader to envision him- or herself in this environment. Once the reader is able to picture him- or herself in this beautiful Caribbean Sea setting, Davis skillfully introduces the book's content.

Figure 1.1 Key Actions Introductions Perform and Why they are Important

Action Performed by Introduction	Why the Action is Important
1. Engage the reader	Authors want to "hook" their readers by immediately grabbing their attention. When an introduction to a piece of informational writing engages a reader, she or he will want to continue reading the work.
2. Introduce key content	A strong introduction will clearly convey to the reader the topic of a particular work and some basic (yet still important) facts about that topic. This information allows readers to clearly understand the text's focus.

Figure 1.2 How the Introduction to *Coral Reef* Performs the Key Actions of an Introduction

Action Performed by Introduction	Section of *Coral Reef* that Performs This Action
1. Engage the reader	"The waters of the Caribbean Sea are warm and clear. On the surface, everything appears peaceful."
2. Introduce key content	"But just below, rising from the bottom of the sea, there is a very busy place. It is the underwater community of the coral reef."

In the third and fourth sentences of this paragraph, Davis transitions from language meant to engage readers to introductory information about the book's content. The third sentence, "But just below, rising from the bottom of the sea, there is a very busy place" shifts the reader's attention away from the water's surface, while the fourth sentence focuses readers specifically on "the underwater community of the coral reef." After reading this paragraph, the reader clearly understands that Davis' book will focus on coral reefs. However, Davis' introduction does more than simply say, "This text is about coral reefs"; it begins by drawing the reader in with an appealing sensory description of the Caribbean Sea and then transitions from that opening image to a specific mention of coral reefs, the book's focal topic. Figure 1.2 highlights the features of this introduction, identifying the two key actions performed by introductions and which components of Davis' text perform each of these actions (a blank, reproducible version of this chart that you can use in your classroom is included in the appendix).

In the next section, we'll take a look inside a third-grade classroom where I helped students understand the importance of crafting an effective introduction.

A Classroom Snapshot

It's a Wednesday morning, and the third graders I'm working with are absolutely humming with energy. They spill into the classroom and take their seats, looking up at the question I've written on the whiteboard: "How would informational texts be different without their introductions?"

This is my third class working with these students on the importance of introductions to informational writing. In our first meeting, I showed students examples of especially effective introductions in published informational texts. During our second meeting, I talked with the students about the key actions introductions perform, using charts such as those in Figures 1.1 and 1.2 to highlight the purposes of introductions and how published authors achieve those purposes in their works. Today, my students will be enhancing their understandings of the importance of effective introductions by considering how published informational texts would be different without their introductions. The goal of this lesson is to further increase students' awareness of why well-crafted introductions are important components of strong informational texts.

I ask someone to read the day's "Big Question" out loud, and a young lady in the front of the room quickly complies. After she reads the question, I explain that it represents the focus for the day's work. "Today, we'll work together to answer this question: 'How would informational texts be different without their introductions?' To figure this out, we'll look together at an example of a published informational text. We'll first look at this example as it was originally written—with its introductory paragraph—and then we'll examine how it would look without this introductory paragraph. After we do this, we'll come back to our Big Question of the day and think about how this published informational text would be different if it didn't have its introduction."

The students nod, and I direct their attention to a section of text from Caroline Arnold's (1980) informational work, *Electric Fish*, which I've projected to the front of the room. The selection I share with the students, which contains the book's opening paragraph and the first few sentences of the second paragraph, looks like this:

> Did you know that an electric eel can produce enough electricity to shock a horse? Did you know that a shark is able to find a fish hidden in the sand because it can feel a small amount of electricity given off by the fish? Did you know that some fish can "talk" to each other with electric signals? All of these fish have a unique sensitivity to electricity.
>
> Some fish can produce an electric current. The electricity is made by a special part of the fish's body called an "electric organ." The electric organ can be very big or very small. (pp. 3–4)

I read the passage out loud, asking the students to follow along. Once I've finished reading it, I ask the students what they noticed about the introduction: "What works about this introductory paragraph? Think back to our conversations about the key actions introductions perform."

"It gets your attention," responds one student, a young man seated at one of the back tables. "The questions at the beginning get you interested."

"Yeah!" interjects another student. "Like the part about the eel being able to shock a horse. That got my attention. It would take a lot to shock a horse!"

"Great job, both of you," I reply. "This introductory paragraph definitely grabs us and gets us to pay attention. Remember that we talked about introductions doing two key things—getting the reader's attention and introducing key content, like the main information the book will discuss. Do you think this introductory paragraph introduces key content?"

Hand shoot up around the room. I call on a young lady, who explains, "I think it does. It talks about fish and electricity, and that's what the book is about."

"Very good point," I respond. "This book is definitely about fish and electricity, and this opening paragraph clearly shows that. It introduces the key content that some fish have a unique sensitivity to electricity."

"Now," I continue, "I'm going to ask you to think about what the opening of this book, *Electric Fish*, would look like if it didn't have its introductory paragraph."

I place the chart in Figure 1.3 on the document camera so that the text projected to the front of the room now contains the original beginning of *Electric Fish* as well as a revised version of the beginning of the book without the introductory paragraph.

I read both versions out loud and ask the students to follow along silently as I do so. Once I finish, I ask the students to connect back to the day's "Big Question" by considering the following question: "How is the beginning of *Electric Fish* different without its introductory paragraph?"

I call on a young lady who has quickly raised her hand. "The introductory paragraph gets you interested and shows what the book's going to be about," she explains. "The part on the right, without the [introductory] paragraph, doesn't do those things. It just dives right in."

Figure 1.3 Original Beginning of *Electric Fish* and a Revised Beginning with the Introductory Paragraph Removed

Original Beginning	Revised Beginning with the Introductory Paragraph Removed
Did you know that an electric eel can produce enough electricity to shock a horse? Did you know that a shark is able to find a fish hidden in the sand because it can feel a small amount of electricity given off by the fish? Did you know that some fish can "talk" to each other with electric signals? All of these fish have a unique sensitivity to electricity. Some fish can produce an electric current. The electricity is made by a special part of the fish's body called an "electric organ." The electric organ can be very big or very small (pp. 3–4).	Some fish can produce an electric current. The electricity is made by a special part of the fish's body called an "electric organ." The electric organ can be very big or very small (pp. 3–4).

"That's really well said," I reply. "Without the introductory paragraph, this book just dives right in. The author doesn't get a chance to grab our interest and introduce us to the topic like she does in the original version. So, how do you think informational texts would be different without their introductions?"

"Without the introduction," answers a student, "the text would just start talking about the topic without getting us interested or showing us what the book is about. The introduction's kind of like the beginning of a movie when they first show you the characters and what's going on. The movie would be confusing if it didn't have that beginning."

I smile, thrilled with the student's comparison: "Excellent connection—I love that comparison you made! Introductions are really important aspects of informational writing. All of you did a great job today of thinking about this. In our next class, we'll work on crafting our own introductions to the informational texts that we'll be writing."

Recommendations for Teaching Students about Introducing a Topic

In this section, I describe a step-by-step instructional process to use when teaching students about introducing a topic in informational writing. The instructional steps I recommend are: 1) Show students examples of introductions from published informational texts; 2) Talk with students about the key actions introductions perform; 3) Ask students to consider how published informational texts would be different without their introductions; 4) Work with students as they craft their own introductions to informational texts; and 5) Help students reflect on why their introductions are important components of their informational writings. Each of these recommendations is described in detail in this section.

1.   Show students examples of introductions from published informational texts.

I view this mentor text use as the foundation of effective writing instruction. By showing our students examples of outstanding introductions, we are allowing them to learn about effective writing directly from expert informational authors. The examples featured in this chapter from *Reptiles, Coral Reef,* and *Electric Fish* are excellent models of introductions and can certainly be used successfully in many classes. However, I also recommend that you keep your students' particular interests in mind when selecting mentor texts to share with them. I have found that when students interact with examples that align with their interests, they are especially likely to be receptive to instruction related to those examples. Once you've shown your students examples of effectively written introductions from published texts, you can think about the next step of this process: considering the key actions that introductions perform.

    2.   Talk with students about the key actions introductions perform.

This next step is firmly rooted in this book's toolkit approach. Now that the students have seen examples of strong introductions, we teachers can talk with them about why introductions are important tools for effective writing. In order for students to understand the importance of a strongly written introduction to an exemplary piece of writing, they must understand the key functions of introductions: 1) Engage the reader; and 2) introduce key content. To help students understand these actions that introductions perform, I recommend beginning by showing them the chart depicted in Figure 1.1. This chart describes each of the actions introductions perform and explains why these actions are important.

Once you have discussed this chart with your students and you are comfortable with their understandings, talk with them about how a published text performs these functions. To do this, present your students with an introduction from a published work and ask them to comment on which sentences from the text are used to engage the reader and which are used to introduce key content. I recommend showing your students an example of your analysis of a text before asking them to do the same on their own. I like to show my students the information in Figure 1.2 so that they can see how I've divided the introduction of Gary Davis' *Coral Reef* into these categories. Once I've discussed this example with my students and am comfortable with their understandings, I release more of the responsibility onto them. I divide the students into small groups, give each group a blank version of the chart depicted in Figure 1.2, and ask each group to fill out the chart by first finding an informational text with an effective introduction and then identifying components of that introduction that are used to engage the reader, as well as other components used to introduce key content. This activity helps students look carefully at published introductions and allows them to consider the ways the authors of these introductions engage the reader and introduce important information.

    3.   Ask students to consider how published informational texts would be different without their introductions.

Now that you've talked with your students about the key actions introductions perform, the next step is to make this instructional process even more interactive by asking students to consider how published informational texts would be different without their introductions. The classroom snapshot described in this chapter provides an example of this instructional recommendation in action—in the snapshot, I showed a third-grade class the original beginning of Caroline Arnold's book *Electric Fish*, as well as how the beginning of that book would look with the introductory paragraph removed. The goal of this activity is to get students to see the importance of the introductory paragraph. When I conduct this activity with students, my objective is to help them understand that without the introductory paragraph, the author wouldn't engage the reader and introduce the key content—instead, the work would simply begin by giving facts to the reader. A student quoted in the snapshot demonstrated an excellent understanding of the importance of introductions to effective informational writing by drawing a comparison to the structure of a movie: "Without the introduction, the text would just start talking about the topic without getting us interested or showing us what the book is about. The introduction's kind of like the beginning of a movie when they first show you the characters and what's going on. The movie would be confusing if it didn't have that beginning."

4.   Work with students as they craft their own introductions to informational texts.

The next step of this instructional process is to release even more responsibility onto the students by asking them to craft their own introductions to informational texts. Before I ask students to begin work on these introductions, I remind them that their introductions should both engage the reader and introduce key content. Once the students begin working, I meet with them individually and talk with them about their progress. I ask students to share with me how their introductions will engage the reader and introduce important information about the piece's topic.

I recently worked with a student who was writing an introduction to an informational piece on Mars. He explained to me that he wanted to engage the reader by capitalizing on the curiosity many people have about Mars' residents. He told me that he believes "Lots of people wonder about Mars. They wonder if anything lives there and if there are really Martians." He continued to explain that he would "begin by asking about Martians because [doing that] can get the reader interested." After that, he explained, he would "introduce some important information about Mars." Impressed by this student's ideas and goals, I told him that I was excited to see the introduction that he creates. This student's introduction is depicted in Figure 1.4.

This introduction does a great job of engaging the reader by asking questions like "Have you ever seen little green aliens on television and wondered, 'Do those things really live on Mars?'" It also transitions effectively from its opening questions to the piece's topic with statements such as, "We don't know if there are really Martians, but scientists have learned

Figure 1.4 Student Introduction about Mars

Have you ever wondered if Martians exist? Have you ever seen little green aliens on television and wondered, "Do those things really live on Mars"? I know I have! Have you ever wondered if people who live on earth could someday live on Mars? Scientists have sent rovers to Mars to find out more about it. We don't know if there are really Martians, but scientists have learned a lot of information about Mars.

a lot of information about Mars." After reading this introductory paragraph, a reader can feel engaged in the topic and ready to read more about Mars. Once students have created these introductions, they can move to the final step of this instructional process, in which they reflect on the importance of introductions to their works.

5. Help students reflect on why their introductions are important components of their informational writings.

To guide the students as they do this, I ask them to reflect on the question, "How does your introduction strengthen your piece of informational writing?" Asking students this question encourages them to think metacognitively (Flavell, 1979) about the significance of introductions to the works they've created and helps them see introductions as important tools that can enhance the effectiveness of informational writing. The student who crafted the previously described introduction to a piece about Mars explained that his introduction enhanced his piece because "it can get the reader really interested." He expanded on this idea by saying, "I asked questions about Martians and about living on Mars. Those questions can make the reader think about the answers and want to know even more about Mars. It can make them curious, and if they're curious, they'll want to read more." This student's response shows an excellent understanding of how an effective introduction can arouse a reader's curiosity and encourage that reader to want to read more of the piece.

Final Thoughts on Introducing a Topic

♦ Introducing a topic when writing informational text is addressed in Common Core Writing Standards W.3.2a, W.4.2a, and W.5.2a.
♦ An introduction to a piece of informational writing is an opening section of one or more paragraphs that provides a brief "first look" at subject matter that will be further developed later in the text.

- ◆ Introducing a topic is important to effective informational writing because a well-crafted introduction performs two key actions:
  - ◆ Engage the reader
  - ◆ Introduce key content.
- ◆ A strong introduction to a piece of informational writing opens the work in a clear and purposeful way that shows the author's ability to capture the reader's attention while also conveying basic information about the book's topic.
- ◆ When teaching students about introducing a topic:
  - ◆ Show students examples of introductions from published informational texts.
  - ◆ Talk with students about the key actions introductions perform.
  - ◆ Ask students to consider how published informational texts would be different without their introductions.
  - ◆ Work with students as they craft their own introductions to informational texts.
  - ◆ Help students reflect on why their introductions are important components of their informational writings.

2

Grouping Related Information Together

What Does "Grouping Related Information Together" Mean?

It is important that authors of informational texts group related pieces of information together. The Common Core Writing Standards address the importance of this concept—Standards W.3.2a, W.4.2a, and W.5.2a emphasize that students should logically and coherently group related pieces of information together when crafting informational writings. In this chapter, we'll discuss the following: what "grouping related information together" means, why this concept is important for effective informational writing, a description of a lesson on this concept, and key recommendations for helping your students effectively group information together in their own informational writing.

Let's begin by examining what it means to group related pieces of information together. When authors of informational texts present information to their readers, they use organizational tools like chapters, sections, and paragraphs to convey this information clearly and logically. To illustrate this, let's take a look at the grouping of information in Darlene R. Stille's (2004) book, *Cheetahs*. Stille divides her book into chapters, such as "The Cheetah's Body," "Where Cheetahs Live," and "How Cheetahs Live." These chapters provide the reader with an initial sense of organization, as they group distinct types of information about cheetahs into different sections of the book. A reader can look at the list of chapters on the book's table of contents page and see that she or he can turn to page 6 to read the chapter on "The Cheetah's Body," to page 12 to find the chapter on "Where Cheetahs Live," and to page 16 to locate the chapter on "How Cheetahs Live."

While these chapters enhance the organization in this book, they are not the only tool Stille uses to group related information together. Within each chapter, Stille organizes information about cheetahs into paragraphs; these paragraphs contain focused information about a specific topic related to that chapter's overall focus. For example, within the chapter, "The Cheetah's Body," Stille includes the following paragraph, which focuses on the way the structure of the cheetah's body enhances the animal's speed:

> The cheetah's body is built for speed. It has long, thin legs that help it run fast. Its spine acts like a spring to help it leap forward. It has claws that act like spikes on running shoes to keep it from slipping. It also has a large heart and large blood vessels. These give its body the oxygen it needs to run fast. (p. 9)

In this paragraph, Stille focuses on a specific aspect of the cheetah's body. Other paragraphs in the same chapter address other components of the cheetah's body, such as the colors and patterns on its coat and the structure of its teeth. The combination of these chapters and paragraphs allows Stille to group related information together when discussing cheetahs.

Why Grouping Related Information Together Is Important to Effective Informational Writing

Grouping related information together is an important component of effective informational writing; by grouping related information together, authors of informational texts can help their readers: 1) Find important pieces of information; and 2) Be sure they have located all of the information on that topic in the text. Let's examine each of these concepts individually.

Grouping Related Information Together Helps Readers Find Important Pieces of Information

By grouping related information together, authors help their readers find important pieces of information. Organizing an informational text into chapters, sections, and paragraphs allows readers to navigate it much more easily than if the text was not organized in those ways. Since many informational texts address broad topics, a strong sense of organization is especially important to readers as they seek to locate specific pieces of information within the piece. For example, Anne Millard's (1996) book *Pyramids* makes a broad topic easily navigable by grouping together distinct types of information on pyramids and clearly conveying that sense of organization through chapters, sections, and paragraphs. One section of this book focuses specifically on the pyramids of Giza and contains information focused solely on this topic, such as the following details: "The pyramids at Giza were built by Khufu, his son Khafre, and grandson Mekaure. Khufu's, the Great Pyramid, is the largest. It is 482 feet (147 m) tall and built with about 2,300,000 blocks" (p. 26).

Since the information in this section focuses only on the pyramids of Giza, readers can clearly distinguish it from other parts of the text that provide information about other pyramids. Because different sections of this book focus on particular topics, readers can easily navigate the text and make sense of its information. Imagine how different a reader's experience with this text would be if there were no sections, chapters, or paragraphs. If this were the case, a reader who wanted to know about the Giza pyramids would have to read through one long passage until he or she found information about Giza. If the text needed to be read this way, it would be far less effective at clearly conveying information and would certainly frustrate the reader! By grouping related information about specific pyramid types together, Millard provides readers with a clear and organized text that provides easy-to-navigate information about its topic. Now, let's take a look at another reason grouping related information together is important: it ensures readers that they have located all of the information on a topic.

Grouping Related Information Together Ensures Readers that They Have Located All of the Information on that Topic in the Text

When authors clearly group information together, they allow readers to be sure that they have located all of the information the text has to offer on a particular topic. To illustrate the importance of this, consider this situation: you're reading through Anne Millard's book *Pyramids* and you want to find all of the information the book contains about the Giza pyramids. Since related pieces of information in this book are grouped together, you can look for the section that describes these pyramids and be sure that all of the book's information about the Giza pyramids is found in this section. If this book was not organized this way, your experience trying to find all of its information about the pyramids of Giza would be much different—and much more difficult! You might locate some information about these pyramids, but, if the author did not group all of the related information together, you wouldn't know for sure if there was more information about the Giza pyramids somewhere else in the book. You would need to read through the entire book to ensure that you had located all of the information on this topic!

As this discussion of *Pyramids* is designed to illustrate, when authors group related information together, readers can easily find important information and be sure that they have located all of the information on that topic contained in the text. If authors of informational text did not group related material together, their works would be very difficult to navigate. This component of informational writing contributes to a piece's organization and makes the work user friendly for readers. Next, we'll take a look at a description of an activity I did with a class of fourth graders that was designed to help these students understand the importance of grouping related information together when writing informational texts.

A Classroom Snapshot

I begin today's class by telling my third graders, "You all have been doing a great job thinking about grouping related information together when writing informational texts. Today, I'm going to show you something that's going to help you understand this concept even better. Are you ready?"

The students enthusiastically reply "Yes!" and "I'm ready!"

These third graders and I are in our third class dedicated to examining the importance of grouping related information together. In our first class on this topic, I showed them examples of published informational writings, highlighting the ways authors grouped related pieces of information together. When we talked about this concept for the second time, our discussion focused on its importance and highlighted the ways grouping related information together helps readers find important pieces of information and allows them to be sure they have located all of the information on that topic in the text.

In today's class, we're going to take a look at a paragraph from a published informational text that focuses on one topic and then compare that example to an informational paragraph that does not focus on a particular topic. After reading both of these paragraphs, we'll reflect on our experiences interacting with these examples.

"Great!" I respond. "I'm glad you're ready! First, let's do a quick review. Can someone remind us of a reason why grouping information together when writing informational text is an important thing to do?"

A number of hands shoot into the air. I call on a student who explains, "It helps readers find information."

"That's right," I tell the student. "When writers group related information together, it becomes much easier for readers to find information. You can look for a chapter, section, or paragraph that relates to the information you're looking for. We also talked about another reason why it's important that writers group information together. Can anyone remind us what that one is?"

I call on another student who says, "It makes it so that we know we found all the information [on that topic]."

"Very good," I reply. "When writers group related information together, readers can be sure they've found all of the information on a certain topic that a piece has to offer. For example, a book on sharks might be organized in sections, with each section focused on a different kind of shark. If there was one specific section on tiger sharks, you could be sure that, once you finished that section, you would have read everything the book had to say about tiger sharks. You wouldn't have to keep looking for more information because the author grouped all of the information about tiger sharks into one section."

The students nod, clearly grasping these ideas, so I move ahead to today's focus: "Now, let's get to what I told you I'd show you. First, I'm going to show you a paragraph from the book *African Animals* by Caroline Arnold (1997). I'm going to ask you to think about whether you think the writer of this book groups related information together when she writes."

I place the following paragraph on the document camera, projecting it to the front of the classroom:

> Elephants are the heaviest of all land animals. Some adults weigh more than fourteen thousand pounds. That's as much as a medium-sized truck! Because elephants are so big, other animals cannot easily harm them. (p. 14)

I read the paragraph aloud, asking students to follow along silently. Once I finish the paragraph, I ask the class: "Is the information in this paragraph related?"

I call on a student sitting in the front of the room, who responds, "Yeah, it's related." When prompted to explain why she feels that way, the student answers, "All of the information is about elephants."

"Great job," I respond. "So would you all say that this author is doing a good of grouping related information together?"

Students around the room call out "Yes!" and nod their heads.

"Awesome," I reply. "Now I'm going to show you another paragraph about African animals. This one isn't from Caroline Arnold's book—it's one that I made up. After we look at it together, I'm going to ask you if the information in this paragraph is clearly related like Arnold's is."

I place the following text on the document camera:

> You can find zebras living in the African grasslands. An interesting fact about zebras is that every zebra has a unique pattern of stripes. Some species of crocodiles live in Africa near bodies of water. These crocodiles have very sharp teeth, which they use to grab on to other animals and eat them.

After reading the paragraph out loud, I ask the students: "What do you think? Does this paragraph group related information together like the one about elephants does?"

A number of students raise their hands; I call on a young man who explains, "I don't think so. It starts talking about zebras and then just goes into talking about crocodiles."

Another student adds on this comment, saying, "I agree. It definitely talks about two different animals. This is a lot more confusing than the other one that was about elephants."

"Fantastic responses, both of you," I tell the students. "This is definitely an example of what *not* to do. Like we've been discussing, one really important part of informational writing is grouping related information together. Now you can see what happens when writers don't group related information together. Instead of clear, focused paragraphs like the one about elephants from *African Animals*, writers can end up with confusing ones without any real focus like the one I just showed you."

The students nod; I smile, pleased that they're grasping this concept. "Before we finish up," I inform them, "I want to show you a piece of paper with both of these paragraphs on it so that we can really see the differences between a paragraph that groups related information together and one that definitely doesn't." I place the chart depicted in Figure 2.1 on the document camera to highlight the differences in focus between these paragraphs.

After I review these paragraphs with the students, I ask if anyone has any final thoughts on the differences. A young lady raises her hand and shares, "The one about elephants just makes a lot more sense. You read it and you think, 'Here's a paragraph about elephants.' The other one doesn't make sense."

"Yeah," interjects another student. "The second paragraph just looks like someone wrote down some random facts."

"Excellent responses!" I responded. "The paragraph about elephants clearly groups related information together, while the paragraph about zebra and crocodiles clearly doesn't. You all did a fantastic job of commenting on both of these paragraphs and showing your understanding

Figure 2.1 Paragraph Comparison

Paragraph that Groups Related Information Together	Paragraph that Does Not Group Related Information Together
Elephants are the heaviest of all land animals. Some adults weigh more than fourteen thousand pounds. That's as much as a medium-sized truck! Because elephants are so big, other animals cannot easily harm them (Arnold, 1997, p. 14).	You can find zebras living in the African grasslands. An interesting fact about zebras is that every zebra has a unique pattern of stripes. Some species of crocodiles live in Africa near bodies of water. These crocodiles have very sharp teeth, which they use to grab on to other animals and eat them.

of the importance of grouping related information together. In our next class, we'll work together on creating our own informational texts that group related information together like Caroline Arnold's paragraph about elephants does. Great job today!"

Recommendations for Teaching Students about Grouping Related Information Together

In this section, I describe a step-by-step instructional process to use when teaching students about grouping related information together in informational writing. The instructional steps I recommend are: 1) Show students examples from published informational texts of related information grouped together; 2) Discuss with students why grouping related pieces of information together is important; 3) Ask students to compare paragraphs that group related pieces of information together with paragraphs that do not group related information together; 4) Work with students as they attempt to group related information together in their own informational writings; and 5) Help students reflect on why grouping related information together is an important aspect of effective informational writing. Each of these recommendations is described in detail in this section.

1. Show students examples from published informational texts of related information grouped together.

The first step gives students an introduction to this concept and allows them to see how published authors apply it to their own works. When recently working with a third-grade class on this topic, I showed students the examples from Darlene R. Stille's (2004) book *Cheetahs* and Anne Millard's (1996) book *Pyramids* cited earlier in this chapter. I found that showing students these examples helped them grasp the concept of grouping related information together much more quickly and efficiently than simply explaining this idea would. After viewing these examples, one student told me, "I like how you showed us how professional authors [group related information together]. I didn't really understand what this meant at first, but I do now [after seeing examples]." This statement illustrates the power of mentor texts—examining examples of a particular writing strategy allowed this student to grasp a concept much more easily and effectively than listening to a lecture about the strategy.

2. Discuss with students why grouping related pieces of information together is important.

The next step in this instructional process is to discuss with students why grouping related information together is important to effective informational writing. Focusing on the importance of this concept allows students to see the significance of this writing tool. In addition, it transitions logically from the mentor examples the students saw in this first step of this process: now that the students have seen examples of authors grouping related information together, they're ready to think about why this is an important writing concept. When I talk with students about this concept, I emphasize that grouping related information together helps readers: 1) Find important pieces of information; and 2) Be sure they have located all of the information on that topic in the text.

When discussing these ideas with my students, I like to model how my experience reading a text is improved when the author has grouped related information together. To do this, I take a piece of informational writing and comment on the ways the author has grouped information together and how this helps me find important information and feel certain I have located all of the information on that topic. I recently conducted one of these "think aloud" activities (Wilhelm, 2001) with Fred Ramen's (2005) book, *North America before Columbus*. Since this book provides information about a number of Native American tribes, I highlighted the ways the author groups related information about these different tribes together. I pointed out that Chapter Four of the book focuses specifically on "Native Tribes of the Southwest" (p. 29) and then called the students' attention to the fact that the chapter is further divided into separate sections—for example, one section in the chapter focuses specifically on the Pueblo tribes, while another addresses the Navajo and the Apache. Within these sections, the author uses paragraphs to further group specific pieces of information. For example, one paragraph in the Pueblo section focuses on secret rituals:

> Great secrecy was attached to Pueblo rituals. Each village had its own interpretation of the rites to be followed. The men who performed the ceremonies were members of secret societies that only slowly revealed their rituals to the younger men of the tribe. (p. 31)

As I identified these ways of grouping related information together, I commented on how they improved my experience as a reader. I told the students, "This author groups information into chapters, and then into sections, and then finally into paragraphs. Because of this, it's pretty easy for me to find the information I'm looking for. It would be a lot harder to find this information on secret Pueblo rituals if the author didn't group related information in these ways."

3. Ask students to compare paragraphs that group related pieces of information together with paragraphs that do not group related information.

The next step in this instructional process is to ask students to compare paragraphs that group related information together with those that do not. This activity, an example of which is described in detail in this chapter's classroom snapshot, is designed to be an interactive discussion in which teachers show students an example of a paragraph that focuses on a singular topic and another paragraph that does not. I like to show students a published paragraph for the correct example and then share with them a version I created as a counter-example. In the classroom snapshot, for example, I showed my students a paragraph from Caroline Arnold's (1997) book *African Animals*; this paragraph focuses exclusively on elephants and is a great example of an author grouping related information together. Then, I showed the students a paragraph I created that discusses both zebras and crocodiles. As I told my students, the paragraph I created is an example of what *not* to do, as it does not group related information together. I find this activity to be effective because it allows students to clearly see the difference between paragraphs that effectively group related information and those that really should be separated into distinct paragraphs. As students move closer to applying this idea to their own writing, it is important that they develop a clear understanding of exactly what grouping related information together looks like; this activity can help provide that understanding.

4. Work with students as they attempt to group related information together in their own informational writings.

The next step in this instructional process releases more responsibility onto the students by asking them to focus on grouping related information together in their own informational works. This places more ownership on students and supports them as they apply this concept to their writings. When I do this with my students, I confer with them individually as they focus on writing their informational texts. In these conferences, I ask the students to show me specific examples of how they've grouped related information together in their pieces. For example, I recently worked with a student who was writing an informational piece on the Arctic tundra. She explained the specific ways she grouped different types of information about the Arctic tundra together: "In the different paragraphs in my paper, I write about different things about [the Arctic tundra]. There's a paragraph about the location, another paragraph about the animals that live there, and another paragraph about the weather." This student continued to say that, as she found more information about the tundra, she would create new paragraphs for different types of information. When conducting these conferences with your students, I recommend asking them to explain how they've grouped related information together in their works. You can then make suggestions when necessary, while still allowing students to feel ownership of the piece.

5. Help students reflect on why grouping related information together is an important aspect of effective informational writing.

The final step of this instructional process is to help students reflect on why grouping related information together is important to effective informational writing. To do this, I like to give students the following response questions to consider: 1) How did grouping related information together make your piece of informational writing as strong as possible?; and 2) What might your piece have been like if you didn't group related information together? These questions require students to reflect on their own works and think about why the writing strategy of grouping related information together is important. I asked the student described in the previous recommendation these questions, and she stated, "Grouping related information together made my paper real strong because it was organized and easy to understand. If you were reading this paper, you'd get to the paragraph about animals in the Arctic tundra and say, 'Oh, I'm going to learn about animals in this paragraph.' If I didn't group related information together, you wouldn't know what you were going to get in each paragraph. It would just all be thrown together." This student's response shows excellent awareness of how grouping related information together has a positive impact on her work.

Final Thoughts on Grouping Related Information Together

- ◆ Grouping related information together when writing informational text is addressed in Common Core Writing Standards W.3.2a, W.4.2a, and W.5.2a.
- ◆ When authors of informational texts present information to their readers, they group related pieces of information together so that they can convey this information clearly and logically.
- ◆ Authors use organizational tools like chapters, sections, and paragraphs to group related information together.
- ◆ Grouping related information together is important to effective informational writing because authors of informational texts can help their readers:
  - ◆ Find important pieces of information.
  - ◆ Be sure they have located all of the information on that topic in the text.
- ◆ When teaching students about grouping related information together:
  - ◆ Show students examples from published informational texts.

- ◆ Discuss with students why grouping related pieces of information together is important.
- ◆ Ask students to compare paragraphs that group related pieces of information together with paragraphs that do not.
- ◆ Work with students as they attempt to group related information together in their own informational writings.
- ◆ Help students reflect on why grouping related information together is an important aspect of effective informational writing.

3

Adding Features that Aid Comprehension

What Does "Adding Features that Aid Comprehension" Mean?

Writers of informational texts frequently incorporate features that aid the reader's comprehension process. These features, such as headings, illustrations, photographs, charts, and graphs, can help readers understand the information discussed in the text. The Common Core Writing Standards emphasize the significance of adding features that aid comprehension: Standards W.3.2a, W.4.2a, and W.5.2a call for students to integrate these kinds of features into their informational writing. In this chapter, we'll discuss the following: what "adding features that aid comprehension" means, why this concept is important for effective informational writing, a description of a lesson on this concept, and key recommendations for helping your students effectively add features that aid comprehension to their own informational writing.

First, let's think further about what it means for a writer to add features that aid a reader's comprehension. Oftentimes, writers of informational texts will give their readers more than a great deal of text about a topic—they may also provide readers with headings, photographs, illustrations, charts, and graphs that help them understand the topic. Different authors will select specific features to include in their works based on the specific topics they are addressing and the particular ways they are describing them. When I read a piece of informational text, I use the text's features to enhance my reading experience: I examine charts, graphs, illustrations, and photographs to increase my understanding of important information, and I read the text's headings to help me identify and understand the specific topics in the piece.

In the book *Symbiosis* (1998), authors Alvin Silverstein, Virginia Silverstein, and Laura Silverstein Nunn use a variety of features to help readers understand the information discussed in the text. For example, they use section headings to divide longer chapters into manageable chunks and clearly communicate to the reader what specific topics are being addressed at particular times. In a chapter called "Microhelpers," which focuses on microorganisms, the authors use the following section headings to guide readers as they move through the chapter: "Making Food Useful" (p.11), "Plants that Need Fixing" (p. 15), and "Good Fungi" (p. 16). Silverstein, Silverstein, and Nunn also use photographs to aid the reader's comprehension. In a section that describes the symbiotic relationship between green algae and giant clams, the authors include a photograph of a giant clam with green algae growing on it. This photograph, which is accompanied by the caption, "Green algae will grow on several of these giant clams, which will use the algae for food" (p. 37), provides readers with a clear visual of what green algae growing on a giant clam looks like; this visual can help readers who might be struggling to grasp the symbiotic relationship between these two entities.

Finally, the authors of this book use text boxes—images inserted into the main text of the book or on the side margin of a page—to provide extra facts about an important issue. For example, in the book's concluding chapter, the authors insert a text box titled "Career Watch: Symbiosis" that discusses the role the study of symbiosis plays in various careers; the authors call attention to the field of ecology with the statement: "Ecology: Studies of symbiotic relationships and their interaction with the environment; genetic engineering to make positive relationships more effective and suppress parasites" (p. 53). The information included in this text box provides readers with additional information about the importance of symbiosis and helps them further their understanding of this concept. In the next section, we'll examine in more detail why features that aid comprehension are important components of effective informational writing.

Why Adding Features that Aid Comprehension Is Important to Effective Informational Writing

Now that we've considered different ways authors add features that aid comprehension, let's think about why doing so is important to effective informational writing. Features such as headings, photographs, illustrations, charts, and graphs help readers maximize their understanding of particular topics. In the book *Symbiosis*, discussed in the previous section, the authors' use of headings, illustrations, and text boxes aid readers in their efforts to understand the concept of symbiosis as fully as possible. If these features weren't used, the book would still get its essential point across, but it would not do so as effectively. When describing the importance of these features to my students, I draw a comparison with the experience of watching a sporting event on television. If I was watching a football game on television that did not have any announcers or graphics telling me the score of the game or how much time was left, I would still have a fundamental understanding of the game. However, these extra features added by the network broadcasting the game—the announcers' commentary, the score of the game, and the amount of time remaining—maximize my understanding of what's happening in the game and why. The same is true of features that aid comprehension: they enhance readers' understandings of a topic and allow them to make sense of a text as effectively as possible.

In this section, we'll consider the features that aid comprehension present in Mary Ellen Snodgrass' (1991) book *Air Pollution* and discuss why these features are important to the text. This book uses section headings, photographs, and illustrations to complement the main text and help readers comprehend the information in the book. Let's take a look at these features individually and consider why each one is important to a reader's attempt to understand the text.

Section Headings

All of the chapters in *Air Pollution* include headings, which divide the chapters into separate sections. In the book's fourth chapter, which addresses the topic "Cleaning the Air," Snodgrass uses the following section headings: "Stopping Air Pollution at Home" (p. 31), "Making Our Nation a Better Neighbor" (p. 32), "Reducing Pollution from Cars" (p. 34), and "Making Safer Factories" (p. 34). These headings are important because they provide readers with a guide to the specific pieces of information that will be addressed in this chapter. While the chapter's title, "Cleaning the Air," gives readers basic information about the topic that the chapter addresses, these section headings provide much more precise information about the material described in the chapter. In addition, these headings show readers how the author has sequenced the subtopics in the chapter. The headings indicate that the chapter first addresses "Stopping Air Pollution at Home" before then moving on to other topics. As readers work through the text, they can see when the author has completed her discussion of one topic and moved on to the next.

Photographs

Mary Ellen Snodgrass also consistently uses photographs in *Air Pollution* to help readers understand important concepts. These photographs complement the book's text by showing readers real-life images of topics it addresses. For example, a section in the book that describes the pollution produced by power plants is accompanied by a photograph of smoke emitted through a power plant's smokestack. Underneath the photograph is the caption, "Generators from power plants can produce strong gases that escape through smokestacks, causing serious threats to clean air" (p. 21). This photograph is important because it shows readers exactly what the smoke produced by power plants looks like, adding a level of specificity to the book. If this photograph were not included, Snodgrass would still make her main point about the pollution produced by power plants, but readers would not get the clear and specific visual made possible by the inclusion of a photograph.

Illustrations

In addition to the section headings and photographs present in *Air Pollution*, Mary Ellen Snodgrass includes illustrations to enhance the reader's comprehension of important ideas. These illustrations correspond with significant topics discussed in the text and explain these concepts in additional detail. For example, a passage that focuses on internal combustion engines is aligned with an illustration that shows the reader what an internal combustion engine looks like and how exhaust is emitted from one of these engines. Because this illustration provides readers with a strong visual awareness of the parts of an internal combustion engine and how one works, it incorporates information that would be much harder to include if only text was used. By adding an illustration of an internal combustion engine, Snodgrass allows the reader to understand the features of this engine as clearly as possible.

As this discussion of the book *Air Pollution* indicates, features that aid comprehension can play important roles in readers' experiences with an informational text. Even though the text would still convey its basic ideas without them, these features help readers understand the main concepts addressed in the book in as much clarity and specificity as possible. In the next section, we'll take a look inside a fourth-grade classroom as the students in that class work on adding features that aid comprehension to their own informational works.

A Classroom Snapshot

I walk into a fourth-grade classroom and am thrilled by what I notice: students excited to add comprehension-enhancing features to the informational texts they've been writing.

"Is today the day when we're going to add the things we've been talking about to our writing?" asks a student, referring to the act of adding features that aid comprehension to the informational pieces she and her classmates have been composing.

"It absolutely is," I reply, "and I love that you asked me about it. I know you all are going to do a great job!"

These students and I have spent the past few days talking about the importance of including features that aid comprehension in effective informational writing. We began by looking together at different examples of texts that incorporate features such as headings, illustrations, photographs, charts, and graphs so that students could get a sense of how published writers use these tools to facilitate readers' comprehension. Afterwards, we discussed why features such as these are important to effective informational writing, highlighting the ways particular texts use specific features to help readers understand important ideas. Once the students demonstrated strong understandings of what these features are and why they are important, I decided it was time for them to work on using them in their own writing. The students in this class have been composing informational texts about topics of interest to them; today, they're going to begin working on adding features that aid comprehension to these texts.

"As one of our classmates just mentioned," I say, addressing the whole class, "today we're going to focus on adding features that aid comprehension to the informational texts you've been writing." I place the chart depicted in Figure 3.1 on the document camera, projecting it to the front of the room, and tell the students, "I'm going to give each of you one of these charts. As you can see, it asks you to list two features you'll add to your informational text and describe each of those features."

"Once I give each of you a copy of this chart," I tell the students, "I'm going to come around the room and have one-on-one conferences with as many of you as I can. I'll ask you what features you're going to add to your informational text. I'll also ask you to describe these features in

Figure 3.1 Adding Features to Informational Writing (a reproducable version of this chart is available in the appendix)

Feature you will add to your informational text	Description of the feature
1.	
2.	

as much detail as you can. I can't wait to see what all of you come up with!"

After giving the students some time to get started, I begin holding individual conferences with the students. I first sit down with a young man who is working on an informational piece about the animals that live in his community. While this student has told me that he is not usually interested in reading and writing, he is motivated by this project. "I really like writing about this topic," he tells me when I sit down with him. "I like looking at the animals that live around me, so it's cool writing about things that are related to my life like this."

"That's fantastic," I reply. "I'm really happy that you're enjoying working on this. I'm excited to hear about the features you're going to add to your text."

"Sure," responds the student. "First, I'm going to use headings, like a lot of the books we looked at did. I'm writing about a few different kinds of animals that live near me, like deer, foxes, and black bears. I'm going to use headings to show which animals I'm talking about at different times."

"Wonderful," I tell the student. "Using headings is a great idea, especially since you'll be discussing different animals in your piece. What's another feature you'd like to add?"

"The other one is photographs," responds the student. "I'm going to include photographs of deer, foxes, and black bears. I'll include these photos when I'm writing about the different animal types to show things about the animals."

"Good," I reply. "When you add the photographs, try to make sure each photo is showing something specific and important about your topic. For example, if you're talking about how bears sometimes get into people's trash cans, you could accompany that with a picture of a bear in someone's trash." Smiling, I tell the student that it's definitely safer to find these pictures from an online source than to try to take his own pictures of a bear, and we both laugh. "Great job thinking about adding these features," I tell him. "I'm excited to see how your piece looks once you've added them."

Next, I sit down with a student who is writing an informational piece about snow leopards. Much to my delight, she is eager to share with me the features she plans to add to her text. "Snow leopards are endangered," she tells me, "and I want to use a chart to show how the amount of snow leopards in the wild is going down."

"That's an excellent use of one of these features," I explain. "You'll be using this chart to make a really important point very clear to the reader. Great idea!"

"Thanks," the student replies, smiling. "I'm also going to use headings."

"What will the headings show?" I inquire.

"I'll have different headings for different things about snow leopards: one heading that says something like, 'How Big Are Snow Leopards?' another that says, 'What Do Snow Leopards Eat?' and other information like that."

"Very nice," I respond. "That will clearly show your reader the specific information about snow leopards you're describing in different sections."

I continue to circulate around the room, conferring with more students about the features they will add to facilitate their readers' comprehension. Once the class period is over, I praise the students' works: "You all did such a great job today. I'm really impressed by the way you thought carefully about the comprehension-aiding features you'll add to your piece and how you'll include these features into your works. We'll keep working on adding these, and I'll keep checking in with you as you finalize these additions. Really nice work!"

Recommendations for Teaching Students about Adding Features that Aid Comprehension

In this section, I describe a step-by-step instructional process to use when teaching students about adding features that aid comprehension. The instructional steps I recommend are: 1) Show students examples of published informational texts containing features that aid comprehension; 2) Discuss with students why specific features that aid comprehension are important to effective informational writing; 3) Have students create their own pieces of informational writing without features that aid comprehension; 4) Ask students to add features that aid comprehension to the pieces they created; and 5) Have students reflect on how the comprehension-enhancing features they added to their works enhanced the quality of their pieces. Each of these recommendations is described in detail in this section.

1. Show students examples of published informational texts containing features that aid comprehension.

The first step in this instructional process is to provide students with mentor examples of published texts that contain features that aid comprehension. Doing so provides students with concrete examples that illustrate the ways published authors integrate comprehension-aiding features into their works. Since there are a number of ways authors can integrate these features into their information, I like to show students a variety of examples. For example, some informational text authors rely primarily on charts and graphs to aid readers' comprehension. Others might feature photographs more prominently, while some others might make use mostly of illustrations. I have found that showing students a range of these possibilities illustrates the options writers have available to them when adding features that aid comprehension. I was recently working with a fourth-grade class on this topic, showing them a variety of ways writers incorporate features that aid comprehension, when a student shared, "I like seeing all of these different things writers do [when adding features that aid comprehension]. It's cool that there's more than one way to do it."

2. Discuss with students why specific features that aid comprehension are important to effective informational writing.

Once you've shown your students examples of the comprehension-aiding features published authors integrate into their works, the next step is to discuss with the students why these features are important to effective informational writing. To do this, I recommend returning to one of the examples you showed the students in the first step of this instructional process and talking with them about exactly how the features in the text enhance the reader's comprehension. For example, I recently conducted such a discussion with fourth graders using an informational text about mummies by Stephen Krensky (2007). This book, titled *The Mummy*, uses section headings, photographs, and illustrations to enhance the reader's comprehension of the text. When discussing each feature with the students, I focused on how it enhances the reader's ability to comprehend the information in the book. When discussing the section headings in the book, I called the students' attention to the heading on page 19, "The Science of Mummification," pointing out to students that this heading helps readers comprehend the text by telling them what specific information is addressed in that section. Within that section, I directed the students to an illustration that reveals how ancient Egyptians prepared bodies for mummification. This illustration is accompanied by the caption, "Ancient Egyptians took great care to properly prepare their dead for the afterlife. In the image below, a priest wraps a dead body in strips of clean linen" (p. 21).

I explained to the students that this illustration enhances a reader's comprehension by allowing readers to see how a priest would wrap a dead body when preparing it for mummification. Since the process of preparing a body for mummification may be unfamiliar to some contemporary readers, the inclusion of this illustration maximizes the reader's understanding. When talking with students about the importance of features that aid comprehension, I emphasized that these features are ways to help readers understand the main concepts addressed in the book as well as possible. "They don't change the message of a piece of informational writing," I explained to the students. "What they do is make the piece of writing as clear and easy to understand as it can be."

3. Have students create their own pieces of informational writing without features that aid comprehension.

The next step of this instructional process is to have students create their own pieces of informational writing—at first, without any features that aid comprehension (those come later!). Creating pieces that initially do not contain features such as charts, graphs, headings, photographs, and illustrations allows writers to first focus on the text itself and the information in it. When I ask my students to create these pieces, I let them know that they will be eventually adding comprehension-aiding features, but their focus at the time is only on creating the text of a piece of informational writing. I like to let students choose their own topics to maximize their sense of ownership of the piece and facilitate their engagement. As students work on these pieces, I conference with them, asking them about their topics and the information they want to convey to the reader. Once the students have composed first drafts of these pieces, we move to the next step of the process, which asks students to add comprehension-aiding features to their pieces.

4. Ask students to add features that aid comprehension to the pieces they created.

The fourth step of this instructional process involves asking students to add features that aid comprehension to the informational texts they created in step 3. This requires students to put their knowledge of this writing tool into action by applying it to their own pieces. As discussed in this chapter's classroom snapshot, I recommend giving students charts to help them brainstorm specific comprehension-aiding features they want to add to their works. The chart I like to use asks the students to identify two features they want to integrate into their informational pieces and to describe each of these features. As the students consider which features to add, I suggest holding one-on-one conferences with them in which you ask them to explain the features they'd like to incorporate. I've found that some students come up with these ideas quickly, while others take more time deciding which features to add to their texts.

If a student is having a difficult time determining which features to use, I begin by asking which of the features we discussed as a class stood out to him or her as effective. If the student is still struggling to come up with effective comprehension-aiding features to use, I take a piece of published informational writing from the school or classroom library and ask the student what he or she notices about its comprehension-aiding features. After examining and discussing these features, students are typically ready to brainstorm comprehension-aiding features they would like to add to their informational works. Once I'm satisfied with the brainstorming my students have done, I ask them to focus on adding the features they've brainstormed to their informational texts. As they do so, I continue to meet with students and monitor their progress. Some students find that the features they initially brainstormed work perfectly, while others decide to integrate even more features than they first brainstormed or to swap one feature for another. For example, I recently conferred with a student who believed he wanted to use illustrations as one of his comprehension-aiding features in an informational piece he was writing about American alligators, but eventually decided that incorporating a chart showing the ways the United States' alligator population varies across states would be most helpful to readers of his work.

5. Have students reflect on how the comprehension-enhancing features they added to their works enhanced the quality of their pieces.

The final step of this instructional process requires students to consider why adding features that aid comprehension is an effective tool for informational writing, and helps students arrive at this understanding by analyzing their own works. To help students reflect on how these features enhanced the quality of their pieces, I ask them to respond to these questions: 1) What features that aid comprehension did you add to your informational writing?; and 2) How can each of these features help readers understand the information in your piece?

I recently discussed these questions with the student described in the previous recommendation who included a chart that shows the states where American alligators live. He explained, "I think this can help people understand the information [in his piece about American alligators] because it shows what states alligators live in and how many live in them. Someone who reads my paper will definitely know where alligators live because of the chart I used. I also wrote about where alligators live, but [the chart] makes this information really clear." This student's reflection reveals his awareness of how the chart he incorporated can enhance a reader's understanding of the American alligator's population distribution. It is especially noteworthy that this student comments on the fact that he also wrote about where American alligators live, but the use of this chart further illustrates and clarifies this idea for the reader. By calling attention to the importance of this chart, this student shows his understanding of how this feature can help readers comprehend his work and indicates his understanding of how features like charts are tools for effective informational writing.

Final Thoughts on Adding Features that Aid Comprehension

- ◆ Adding features that aid comprehension when writing informational text is addressed in Common Core Writing Standards W.3.2a, W.4.2a, and W.5.2a.
- ◆ Writers of informational texts will often give their readers more than a great deal of text about a topic—they also frequently provide readers features such as headings, photographs, illustrations, charts, and graphs that help them understand the topic.
- ◆ Different authors will select specific features to include in their works based on the specific topics they are addressing and the particular ways they are describing them.
- ◆ Features that aid comprehension are important to effective informational writing because they help readers maximize their understanding of particular topics.
- ◆ If features that aid comprehension were not used, a piece of informational writing would still get its essential point across, but it might not be as effective in doing so.
- ◆ When teaching students about adding features that aid comprehension:
  - ◆ Show students examples of published informational texts containing features that aid comprehension.
  - ◆ Discuss with students why specific features that aid comprehension are important to effective informational writing.
  - ◆ Have students create their own pieces of informational writing without features that aid comprehension.
  - ◆ Ask students to add features that aid comprehension to the pieces they created.
  - ◆ Have students reflect on how the comprehension-enhancing features they added to their works enhanced the quality of their pieces.

4

Developing a Topic

What Does "Developing a Topic" Mean?

In order to create effective pieces of informational writing, authors need to develop the topics they address in their works. The Common Core Writing Standards emphasize the significance of this concept, as standards W.3.2b, W.4.2b, and W.5.2b call for students to develop topics in their informational writing. In this chapter, we'll discuss the following: what "developing a topic" means, why it is important to effective informational writing, a classroom snapshot of a fourth-grade class working on this concept, and key recommendations for helping your students effectively develop the topics in their own informational writing.

Let's begin by considering what it means for an author of an informational text to develop a topic. In order to maximize a reader's understanding of a particular topic, authors use information such as facts, definitions, details, quotations, and examples that allow for an in-depth discussion of relevant material. To illustrate this, let's take a look at the ways authors Michael and Mary Woods develop important topics in their book *Tsunamis* (2007). In the following paragraph, the authors of this book develop key ideas for their readers:

> Tsunamis are waves that crash down onto shore and cause disasters. Disasters are events that cause great destruction. Some tsunamis are more than 100 feet (30 m) high. They would reach up to the tenth-floor windows on a skyscraper. Tsunamis can be hundreds of miles long. They can travel thousands of miles at speeds of nearly 600 miles per hour (970 km/hr). That's as fast as jet airplanes fly. (p. 6)

In this passage, Michael and Mary Woods develop the topic of tsunamis in a number of ways: they define "tsunamis" and "disasters," both of which are key terms to this passage, they provide specific facts about the possible height and speed of tsunamis, and they elaborate on these facts by comparing them to well-known entities such as skyscrapers and jet airplanes.

At another point in this book, the authors use specific details to develop their discussion of the impact of the 2004 Indian Ocean tsunami:

> When the water pulled back after the 2004 Indian Ocean tsunami, it left a big mess. More than 500,000 people in southern Asia and eastern Africa had broken bones, cuts, and other injuries. They needed doctors and nurses. But the monster waves had smashed hospitals and doctor's offices. Doctors and nurses also were dead or hurt. (p. 36)

In this excerpt, Michael and Mary Woods provide readers with concrete information about this tsunami's impact. Readers of this passage learn how many people were injured by the tsunami, some types of injuries these people experienced, and why medical care was hard for them to obtain. By including these specific details, these authors develop the topic of the 2004 Indian Ocean tsunami and allow readers to clearly understand its effects.

As these passages illustrate, *Tsunamis* provides excellent examples of informational authors developing important topics. In the next section, we'll consider why developing a topic is an important component of effective informational writing.

Why Developing a Topic Is Important to Effective Informational Writing

Writers develop the topics in their informational works to provide readers with clear understandings of important concepts. Ruth Culham (2003) explains that elaborating on topics and describing them with specific details is important to clearly conveying the ideas in one's writing. If authors of informational texts did not use a great deal of facts, definitions, details, quotations, and examples to develop the topics in their pieces, readers would not fully understand the information being discussed. A piece of informational writing in which key topics were not developed in detail would be frustrating to read, as it wouldn't provide readers with essential understandings they would need to fully make sense of the text. By clearly and explicitly developing the topics in their works, authors of informational texts ensure their readers will learn important details about relevant topics.

In this section, we'll look closely at how Eileen Lucas, author of the informational text *Acid Rain* (1991), develops topics in her work, and we'll reflect on how the development of these topics is essential to the success of this piece. In her book's first chapter, Lucas discusses the concept of acid rain, providing readers with essential information about this topic:

> Acid rain is rain, snow, sleet, or other forms of precipitation that have a higher acid content than normal. Some acids occur naturally in the atmosphere, but many others are the result of human activities. When these acids collect in the atmosphere, they combine with moisture in the air and the result is rain that is sometimes as acid as vinegar. (p. 9)

In this paragraph, Lucas develops the topic of acid rain in a way that is crucial to the reader's understanding of this book. Since acid rain is the focal topic of her book, it is especially important that Lucas discusses this topic and ensures readers develop strong understandings of what it is. Lucas' work in this paragraph certainly contributes to such an understanding: she defines acid rain, describes the process by which it occurs, and explains its potency by informing us that it can contain as much acid as vinegar. If Lucas did not include this paragraph in her book, readers would be without essential information about acid rain. If readers were not provided with this information about the book's central topic, it would be much more difficult for readers to make sense of this text.

At another point in this book, Eileen Lucas develops the topic of fossil fuels, providing readers with important details about this essential concept. Lucas explains:

> Coal, oil, and natural gas are called fossil fuels. They were formed over millions of years from the remains of once-living trees, other plants, and animals. These living things died and fell into the swamps that covered ancient Earth. Year by year, century by century, more living things fell on top of the older ones. Over millions of years, the organic (once living) material was compressed by the weight above it and was gradually changed into the fossil fuels that we now remove from the earth for use in producing energy. (p. 11)

In this excerpt, Lucas describes the history and development of fossil fuels in depth. She incorporates specific information about the objects that eventually became fossil fuels and the process through which this transformation took place. If Lucas did not incorporate all of these specific facts, details, and explanations, readers would not develop the in-depth understanding of fossil fuels that this text facilitates. A much more basic mention of the origin of fossil fuels would not give readers such a concrete and specific awareness of the information addressed in this passage. A bit later in this same chapter, Lucas explains that the substances released when fossil fuels are converted into energy play major roles in the formation of acid rain. By describing the history and development of fossil fuels in so much detail, this author helps readers clearly understand how they originated.

As these excerpts from Eileen Lucas' *Acid Rain* show, developing a topic in detail is important to effective informational writing. If Lucas did not carefully and deliberately develop the concepts of acid rain and fossil fuels in her piece, readers would not be able to understand these topics as clearly. Readers of Lucas' text would not know the definitions of acid rain and fossil fuels, nor would they understand the origins of each of these concepts. When working with our students on this concept, we want for them to develop important topics in their works just as Lucas does in hers. When students use information such as facts, definitions, details, quotations, and examples to describe important topics, they convey their ideas clearly and their readers form strong understandings of the piece's focal concept. In the next section, we'll take a look inside a fourth-grade class and examine an activity I used to help my students understand this concept.

A Classroom Snapshot

I begin today's activity with my fourth graders by pointing at the book-filled shelves all around the classroom and telling the students, "Today, we're going to keep thinking about how writers develop topics in depth, but we're going to do it a little differently. You and your small group members are going to pick an informational text from our classroom library and think about how the author of that book develops a topic in depth. Once you and your group members have thought about this, you'll share your ideas and an example from your book with the rest of the class."

The students nod, appearing interested. This is our third class period discussing the writing concept of developing a topic in depth. In our first session, I showed students what it looks like when published authors develop the topics in their works. In our second class on this topic, we discussed why developing a topic in depth is especially important to effective writing, focusing on why the in-depth information authors provide about key concepts in their works is important to the reader's understanding of the text.

In today's class, the students are going to take an especially active role in their learning. I explain to them that their task is to find an informational text in the classroom library and do the following: 1) Select a passage from the text; 2) Identify the topic addressed in that passage; and 3) Explain what information the author uses to develop this topic. "Remember that authors use all kinds of information to develop topics," I tell the students, "like facts, definitions, details, quotations, and examples. I'm really excited to see what you find. Before you start, though, let's talk together about how you might analyze a passage."

I place a passage from Louise and Richard Spilsbury's (2003) book *Crushing Avalanches* on the document camera, projecting the following text to the front of the room:

> When avalanches hit towns or cities, large numbers of people may face other dangers. The force of an avalanche can trap people under collapsed buildings or inside cars. It can pull down power lines that may electrocute people. Power lines can also make sparks that start fires. (p. 19)

I read the passage out loud and then explain to the students, "As you can see, I've identified this passage from the book *Crushing Avalanches*, just like you'll identify a passage from a book that you select. Now that we've found this passage, the next step is to identify the topic addressed in it. Who would like to tell us what topic this passage addresses?"

Hands fly up around the room; I call on a student who explains, "It's about avalanches."

"That's true," I reply, "but what specific element of avalanches does it focus on?"

"The dangers of avalanches," the same student answers.

"That's great!" I respond. "Great job of identifying the specific topic the passage addresses. Now, let's consider our next question: what information do the authors use to develop this topic?"

Another student explains, "They give a lot of examples. They don't just say people can face dangers; they say the kinds of dangers, like being trapped or being electrocuted, or there being a fire."

"Fantastic work," I tell the student. "You're absolutely right—the authors of this book give specific examples of the kinds of dangers people may face if there is an avalanche. You did an excellent job of listing the specific kinds of dangers these authors identify. Really nice work! Now, you all in your small groups are going to do this same type of analysis. You'll pick an informational text from the classroom library, select a passage, identify the topic addressed in the passage, and be able to explain to the rest of us what information the author uses to develop the topic. After everyone takes some time to do this, each group will share its passage and its thoughts with the rest of the class. I'll come around and meet with you while you work. Go ahead and get started!"

The students begin by combing through the classroom library and selecting texts to use for this activity. After the students have taken a few minutes to look through these texts, I begin to check in with them. I sit down next to one small group and ask the students in that group how they're doing. "We're doing great," one explains. "We picked the book *The Vikings* (Binns, 2005)."

"Very good," I reply. "What passage did you select?"

"This one on page 20. The topic is Viking traders," answers one of the students in the group.

"Great," I respond. "I love that you identified the topic. What information does the author use to develop it?"

"A lot of specific details," states one of the students. "The book says, 'Vikings used their ships to take trade good along the rivers that ran into Russia. They took wax, honey, slaves, and furs to trade for luxuries such as jewelry, wine, silk, and spices.' There are a bunch of details here. The book tells us the things the Vikings took and the things they traded them for. It doesn't just say, 'They traded things.'"

"That's a fantastic analysis," I tell the student. "You did a wonderful job of explaining the way the author develops the topic and giving specific examples of the details the author uses when developing the topic in this way. Wonderful job!"

Next, I meet with a small group that is working with the book *Charles Lindbergh: A Human Hero* by James Cross Giblin (1997). A member of the group eagerly tells me, "We found a really good one!"

"Awesome!" I reply. "Tell me about it."

It's right here," the student says, pointing at page 52 of the book. "This paragraph is about all of the equipment Charles Lindbergh had when he flew on the *Spirit of St. Louis* airplane."

"Very nice," I respond. "How does the author develop this topic?"

"By using a lot of examples," the student replies. This student reads from the book to demonstrate the examples present in this passage:

All the equipment for the flight had been assembled—Charles's flight suit, water canteens, Army rations, a rubber raft, a repair kit, and ref flairs in case the plane went down in the ocean and Charles had to signal from the raft. (p. 52)

"That is definitely a lot of examples," I tell the group. "Why do you think the author used so many of these examples?"

"Because," answers a student in the group, "all of these show the equipment he had. It tells exactly what he brought with him."

I praise this group's work and continue to circulate the classroom, checking in with the remaining groups. Once I've done so, I explain that it's time for each small group to share its insights with the whole class. The first group to volunteer is the group that worked with the book on Charles Lindbergh. A member of this group places the book on the document camera and reads the previously discussed passage about the equipment assembled on the *Spirit of St. Louis*. This student explains, "This section from *Charles A. Lindbergh: A Human Hero* is all about the equipment on his plane, the *Spirit of St. Louis*. The author, James Cross Giblin, develops the topic with examples. He gives a ton of examples of the equipment on this plane. This shows that examples are really important for developing a topic because they provide lots of specific information."

The other groups in the class share their texts and analyses as well. Once they've finished, I commend the students' work: "Excellent job, all of you! I really like the way all of our groups discussed the ways the authors of their pieces develop important topics. Next time, we'll focus on doing this in our own writing!"

Recommendations for Teaching Students about Developing a Topic

In this section, I describe a step-by-step instructional process to use when teaching students about developing a topic in informational writing. The instructional steps I recommend are: 1) Show students published examples of authors developing topics in informational writing; 2) Talk with students about why developing a topic is important to effective informational writing; 3) Have students analyze how published authors develop topics; 4) Ask students to develop the topics in their own works; and 5) Have students reflect on how developing the topics in their own informational writing enhanced their works. Each of these recommendations is described in detail in this section.

1. Show students published examples of authors developing topics in informational writing.

The first step of this instructional process is to show students published examples of authors developing topics in informational writing. Doing this gives students clear understanding of what a sufficiently developed topic looks like, providing a strong foundation for the rest of the work they will do throughout this instructional process. When I show students published examples of this concept, I like to call attention to the many ways to develop a topic by showing students a range of mentor texts in which authors develop their topics in different ways.

When recently working with a group of students on this concept, I showed them an example from Sheila Dinn's (1996) book *Hearts of Gold*— an informational text about the Special Olympics—that develops a topic with a quotation, and one from Stephen Hoare's (1998) book *The World of Caves, Mines, and Tunnels* that uses definitions and details to describe trench warfare in World War I. When discussing *Hearts of Gold*, I showed the students a passage that explains that participating in sports can have a positive impact on young people and pointed out the following quotation from a Special Olympics athlete named Holly Mandy that develops this idea: "Sports lets me be proud of who I am and what I can do . . . plus it shows me what I can do with hard work" (p. 51). When talking about *The World of Caves, Mines, and Tunnels* with the students, I shared with them the following passage about trenches that uses definitions and examples to develop the focal topic:

> Once lines of trenches had been dug, the next most important thing was to excavate living quarters and command posts. These were called "dug-outs" and the miners who were commissioned to do the digging were known as "sappers". They tunneled 35 feet below the level of the trench and reinforced the roof with steel bars, concrete, and sand bags. (p. 28)

Showing students these distinct examples lets them see different ways authors develop the topics in their works. Once students have seen these examples, you can move to the next stage: talking with students about the importance of developing a topic.

2. Talk with students about why developing a topic is important to effective informational writing.

When I discuss this topic with students, I focus on conveying to them that authors develop topics in depth to help readers understand the information being discussed. For example, the passages from *Hearts of Gold* and *The World of Caves, Mines, and Tunnels* described in the previous section would not be very informative if the authors of those passages didn't clearly develop those topics. The quotation in *Hearts of Gold* from a Special Olympics athlete supports and develops the author's point about the positive impact of sports participation, and the definitions and examples used in *The World of Caves, Mines, and Tunnels* to describe trenches allow readers to understand this topic in much more depth. When talking with your students about the importance of developing a topic to effective informational writing, I recommend showing students specific informational texts (you can use the same ones you used in the first step of this instructional process) and thinking aloud about why the information used to develop particular topics is important to the reader's understanding. Thinking aloud in this way will help students grasp the importance of this component of effective informational writing.

3. Have students analyze how published authors develop topics.

The third step in this instructional process is to put more responsibility onto the students by having them analyze how published authors develop topics in their informational pieces. An example of how this step can look in practice is described in this chapter's classroom snapshot: students select an informational text, find a passage in that text in which a topic is described in detail, identify the topic addressed in that passage, and finally explain what information the author uses to develop the topic. I like to have students do this activity in small groups so that they can collaborate with one another and learn from their peers' insights. Before the students begin this activity, I recommend engaging the whole class in an analysis of a text. In this chapter's classroom snapshot, the students and I worked together as a class to analyze an excerpt from Louise and Richard Spilsbury's book *Crushing Avalanches* (2003) before the students worked in small groups with texts of their own choosing. I like to begin with this whole-class example because it gives students a clear understanding of what to do in their small groups and therefore can help them feel prepared and confident when it's time for them to do the activity.

Once the students begin working in their small groups, I recommend meeting with each small group in order to gauge their progress and determine if they need any support. This allows you to talk further with the students about the ways authors develop topics in their works and clarify any confusion they have. When you're satisfied with each group's work, you can ask each group to share its insights with the rest of the class by reading the passage it selected, identifying the topic addressed in that passage, and explaining how the author develops this topic. After a class I taught in which students took part in this activity, one student shared that she benefited from it: "This was really cool. I liked picking a book that my group and I liked and talking about it with the class. It was also cool explaining how the writer of the book developed the topic in the example we picked." This student's insight reveals the engagement and learning that can result from this activity.

4.   Ask students to develop the topics in their own works.

Now that they have analyzed how published authors develop the topics in their works, it's time to place even more responsibility on the students by focusing the attention on their own writing. The fourth step of this instructional process is to ask students to develop the topics in their own informational works. Asking the students to apply this concept to their own writings helps them understand that developing a topic is an important tool for effective writing that all informational writers— including elementary school students!—should apply to their works. When my students and I reach this stage of the instructional process, I have them work independently on their own pieces as I come around the room and confer with them individually. When I confer with the students, I talk with them about the subjects of each of their works, the specific topics within that subject, and the particular ways they are developing those topics. For example, I recently conferred with a fourth grader who was writing an informational piece on snowboarding. He was especially motivated to make this piece as strong as possible because he would be sharing it with his classmates, many of whom also like snowboarding. In one section of the piece, he specifically addressed the topic of famous snowboarder Shaun White. When I asked the student how he would develop this topic, he explained, "I want to put in a lot of details about the different events Shaun White has won, like in the Olympics and the X-Games. Putting in these details will definitely develop the topic because people [who read the paper] will know about all the things Shaun has won and how good he is." This student's explanation shows that he is thinking about specific ways to develop this topic and the impact that including these details about Shaun White will have on the reader.

5. Have students reflect on how developing the topics in their own informational writing enhanced their works.

The final step of this instructional process is to have students reflect on how developing the topics in their informational writing enhanced their works. Doing so helps students further understand the importance of the writing tool of developing a topic, as it requires them to think about how developing the topics in their works made their pieces stronger. To help students reflect on this idea, I ask them to respond to two related questions: 1) How did developing the topics in your piece enhance its effectiveness?; and 2) What would it be like for readers to read your piece if you didn't develop your topics in detail?

I like to ask students to talk about these questions with partners or small group members, citing as many specific examples as possible. After this, I invite volunteers to share their insights with the whole class. When I recently conducted this activity with a class of fourth graders, one of the students who volunteered to share with the class was the previously described student who was writing about snowboarding. When sharing with the class, he addressed the ways he developed a number of topics related to snowboarding, including his discussion of Shaun White: "I wrote about snowboarding and I think developing the topics was really important [to the quality of his paper]. In one part, I talked about Shaun White and gave a lot of details about things he won. If I didn't give those details, it would have been weird, like I was saying he's a great snow-boarder but I couldn't prove it. The details give the proof and show he's great. In another part, I talk about styles of snowboarding, like slopestyle. If I didn't use details about what that is, people who don't know about snowboarding wouldn't understand what I'm talking about." This stu-dent's explanation reveals a strong awareness of why developing these topics is important to the success of his piece. Without the details he uses to develop these topics, his readers would not know the specifics of Shaun White's success, nor would those who are not familiar with the topic understand the specifics of the different styles the piece describes. Developing these topics in depth certainly enhances this student's piece.

Final Thoughts on Developing a Topic

◆ Developing a topic when writing informational text is addressed in Common Core Writing Standards W.3.2b, W.4.2b, and W.5.2b.

◆ Authors develop topics by using information such as facts, definitions, details, quotations, and examples that allow for an in-depth discussion of relevant material.

◆ Writers develop the topics in their informational works to provide readers with clear understanding of important concepts.

◆ If authors of informational texts did not use a great deal of facts, definitions, details, quotations, and examples to develop the topics in their pieces, readers would not fully understand the information being discussed.

◆ When teaching students about developing a topic in informational writing:

  ◆ Show students published examples of authors developing topics in informational writing.

  ◆ Talk with students about why developing a topic is important to effective informational writing.

  ◆ Have students analyze how published authors develop topics.

  ◆ Ask students to develop the topics in their own works.

  ◆ Have students reflect on how developing the topics in their own informational writing enhanced their works.

5

Linking Ideas

What Does "Linking Ideas" Mean?

An important tool used by successful authors of informational text is the writing strategy of linking ideas. The Common Core Writing Standards address the significance of this component of effective writing: Standards W.3.2c, W.4.2c, and W.5.2c each call attention to the importance of linking ideas when crafting informational text. In this chapter, we'll discuss the following: what "linking ideas" means, why this concept is important for effective informational writing, a description of a lesson on this concept, and key recommendations for you to keep in mind when helping your students understand how to link ideas in their own informational works.

First, let's think about what "linking ideas" means. Authors of informational texts frequently describe topics "within and across categories of information" (Common Core State Standards, 2010). This means that sometimes authors will link information and ideas that are similar, as well as those that are different from each other. In either case, it is important that authors link these ideas together to clearly communicate to readers how the ideas relate to one another. When linking ideas, authors use words and phrases such as "also, another, and, because, but, especially, for example," and "in contrast" (Common Core State Standards, 2010). An author might use language such as "for example" to indicate related statements, while using a phrase like "in contrast" to show that two statements differ from one another. In either case, the author would be linking the ideas she or he is conveying to the reader—by revealing the similarities in some situations and indicating the differences in others.

Let's look at an example from a published work in which an author utilizes the concept of linking ideas. In his informational text, *Steam*

Locomotives, Karl Zimmerman (2004) uses language to link key ideas in the following passage, which describes a locomotive called the *John Bull*:

> Though the locomotive was built in Britain, it was in the United States that a warning bell and headlight were added. Also added was a pilot or "cowcatcher," which was attached to the front of the engine and designed to push obstructions, including cattle, off the tracks. (p. 15)

Zimmerman uses the word "also" to link related ideas: after informing the reader of some of the items that were added in the United States to the *John Bull*, he uses "also" to establish a link between these and other items that were added to this locomotive. At another point in *Steam Locomotives*, Zimmerman uses the word "unfortunately" to link ideas in a passage. When describing a locomotive called the *Best Friend*, Zimmerman writes,

> The *Best Friend* was quite a success, hauling as many as five cars with fifty passengers. Unfortunately, about five months after its much-praised debut, the locomotive's fireman tied down its safety valve because the hiss of escaping steam annoyed him. (p. 14)

Through his use of the word "unfortunately," Zimmerman establishes a connection between the passage's opening statement about the success of the *Best Friend* and its subsequent one, which introduces the problems it experienced. This word links the ideas in these two sentences and indicates to the reader that the difficulties described in the second sentence were not desirable (in contrast to the successes discussed in the first sentence). Both of these examples from *Steam Locomotives* illustrate ways Karl Zimmerman links important ideas in his work. In the next section, we'll discuss why linking ideas is especially important to effective writing.

Why Linking Ideas Is Important to Effective Writing

The writing strategy of linking ideas is important to crafting an effective informational text because this strategy clearly communicates to readers how ideas relate to each other. By doing so, the act of linking ideas makes a piece much easier to read and understand than it would be if the ideas were not carefully and skillfully linked. In this section, we'll take a look at some published examples in which authors link ideas, discuss why it is important that these authors did so, and examine how differently the examples would read if the ideas were not linked in these ways.

Let's begin by examining an example from Sandra Markle's (2004) informational book, *Outside and Inside Killer Bees*. In this example, Markle uses the word "however" to link the ideas in two sentences: "An African-ized bee's antennas are even more sensitive than those of European honeybees. However, the antennas of both kinds of bees look the same" (p. 11). Markle's use of "however" connects the ideas in these statements and ensures that readers understand the relationship between them. The first sentence in this excerpt states the differences in the antennas of Afri-canized and European bees, while the second sentence explains that the two types of bees have identical appearances. If the author had not used the word "however" to link these ideas, the excerpt would read like this: "An Africanized bee's antennas are even more sensitive than those of European honeybees. The antennas of both kinds of bees look the same." If the passage were written this way, its basic ideas would still be present, but there would be nothing to link those ideas and establish the relation-ship between them. The word "however" connects these ideas and makes this passage much easier to understand.

Now, let's take a look at another example of an informational text author using language that links ideas. In Daniel Gilpin's (2006) book, *Snails, Shellfish, & Other Mollusks*, he uses the word "also" to link ideas in the following sentences: "Slugs and snails are small, slow-moving, silent creatures. Also, they are most active at night, so they are often overlooked" (p. 26). By using the word "also," Gilpin clearly indicates the relationship these sentences have to each other: both of them are providing the reader with facts about slugs and snails. If Gilpin did not use the word "also" to connect the ideas in these sentences, the text would read, "Slugs and snails are small, slow-moving, silent creatures. They are most active at night, so they are often overlooked." This passage doesn't possess the same clarity and flow that the original version does. By using "also" to link the ideas about slugs and snails in these sentences, Daniel Gilpin ensures that readers have a clear understanding of how these pieces of information relate to each other.

So, why is linking ideas an important element of effective informational writing? The linking of ideas is a tool that writers use to clarify the rela-tionship between the information in particular statements. Words and phrases such as "also, another, and, because, but, especially, for example, in contrast, however" and others allow informational authors to indicate how specific ideas are related. When an author wants to show that the ideas in two statements are distinct from one another, she might use "in contrast" or "however." If that same author desires to show that ideas in two statements are building on each other, she might implement "another" or "for example" to illustrate this. Using these words communicates the relationship between key ideas and helps make the piece as easy to read as possible. Next, we'll take a look inside a fourth-grade classroom and examine how the students in that class work to understand this important concept.

A Classroom Snapshot

I begin today's work with my fourth graders by praising their recent work on the topic of linking ideas: "I'm really impressed with everything you've had to say so far about linking ideas. You're really doing a great job."

"It's pretty fun," volunteers one student.

"Yeah," shares another. "And it seems important. You need to connect things you write about."

Beaming from these responses, I continue, "I'm so thrilled to hear that! Today, we're going to keep thinking about linking ideas, and we're going to do it by considering this question."

I point to the whiteboard, where I've written the question, "How would published informational texts be different if you removed the words that link ideas?" I read the question out loud and explain, "This is what we're going to think about today—how informational texts would be different if we removed the words that link ideas in them." I then explain to the students the activity they'll do in relation to this question. "You're going to get together in your usual groups," I tell them, "and each group is going to pick an informational text from the classroom library. Once you've done those things, I'm going to give you a chart like this one." I place the chart depicted in Figure 5.1 on the document camera so the students can all see it. (A blank version of this chart that you can copy for use in your classroom is available in the Appendix).

"As you can see," I tell the students, "this chart asks you to identify the book you and your group use, an example from that book that contains words or phrases that link ideas, that example rewritten without

Figure 5.1 Template for Linking Ideas Activity Using Published Work

Title and author of the book you used	Example from text that contains language that links ideas	Example rewritten without language that links ideas	Why you think the language that links ideas is important to the original text

the language in the original version that links ideas, and why you think the language that the author used to link ideas is important to the original text. Remember that some of the words and phrases that link ideas that we've discussed recently are also, another, and, because, but, especially, for example, in contrast, and however." While saying this, I point to a piece of chart paper on one of the classroom walls that has these words and phrases listed on it and tell the students, "You can look back at this chart if you need a reminder of some examples while you're working, but also remember that there are other words and phrases authors can use to link ideas."

Before the students begin work on this activity, I tell them that I want to show them an example. "This way, you'll have an even better understanding of what to do while you work on this," I inform them. I place the chart depicted in Figure 5.2 on the document camera.

Figure 5.2 Example of Linking Ideas Activity Using Published Work

Title and author of the book you used	Example from text that contains language that links ideas	Example rewritten without language that links ideas	Why you think the language that links ideas is important to the original text
Sitting Bull by Anne M. Todd	"Sitting Bull's parents named him Jumping Badger, but no one called him by that name. Instead, people called him Hunk-es-ni, which means slow." (p. 9)	Sitting Bull's parents named him Jumping Badger, but no one called him by that name. People called him Hunk-es-ni, which means slow.	The word "instead," which links the ideas in these sentences, is important because it shows how the two sentences are related. "Instead" shows that, even though Sitting Bull's parents named him one thing, other people called him something else. Without that word, the ideas in the sentences aren't clearly connected and the sentences seem choppy.

I talk through the information on this chart with the students, explaining the importance of the word "instead," which links the ideas in this excerpt from Anne M. Todd's (2003) book *Sitting Bull*, and discussing how the version rewritten without "instead" does not connect the ideas in these sentences as clearly. "Now that you've seen this example," I say to the students, "are you ready to do this analysis in your groups?"

"Yeah," a number of students reply. I smile and tell them that I'm excited to see what they come up with.

"While you work," I inform the students, "I'll come around and see how each group is doing." I give each group a chart like the one depicted in Figure 5.1. "Now that you all have a chart to fill out, go ahead and select an informational text from the classroom library to use. After you get started, I'll begin checking in with you."

After several minutes pass, I sit down with a group and ask them how they're doing with this activity. "Good," responds a student in the group, while the others nod agreement.

"Excellent," I reply. "Talk to me about what book you picked and the words you found in it that link ideas."

"Okay," says another student. "We used this book called *The Grizzly Bear* (Silverstein, Silverstein, and Nunn, 1998)," she explains, pointing to the book.

"Yeah," interjects another student in the group. "The example we found of linking ideas is this part here that says, 'When there is a small population of grizzlies, the mating pair will stay together for two to three weeks. However, in a larger population both the male and female may wander off and may have several different mating partners.'" (She points to this passage, located on page 27 of the book, while reading it.) "The word that we thought linked ideas is 'however.' When we rewrote this without 'however,' the ideas definitely weren't linked. When we rewrote it, it said, 'When there is a small population of grizzlies, the mating pair will stay together for two to three weeks. In a larger population both the male and female may wander off and may have several different mating partners.' These sentences don't seem linked now; they just seem like separate sentences. 'However' definitely linked them."

"That's an outstanding analysis!" I exclaim. "You did a really great job of analyzing the way the word 'however' links the ideas in these sentences. I loved the way you identified how different these sentences were when the word 'however' wasn't used. Great job!"

These students smile and fist-bump one another as I move toward another group. I sit down with this group and ask them about their progress. "We just finished up," answers one student in the group. "We used this book here," he says, pointing to the book *If You Lived in Colonial Times* by Ann McGovern (1992).

"Awesome," I reply. "Talk to me about what you found."

"We picked out this section where the author uses the word 'another' to link the ideas," responds another student in the group. The student proceeds to read the following text from page 62 of the book: "If the town crier had special news to tell, he rang a bell or banged on a drum. Then people ran to hear what he was saying. Another way to hear the news was to go to the village inn."

"Nice job of finding that example," I tell the group. "Now, why do you all think 'another' is important to this example?"

"It definitely connects the ideas," answers a student. "The author's talking about the town crier, and then about the village inn. 'Another' connects them."

"Very well said!" I say, praising the student's analysis. "Rewriting this passage without the word 'another' definitely would be different. Like you said, these ideas wouldn't be connected without it."

I proceed to check in with the two other small groups in the class before calling the whole class to attention. "You all did wonderful work today," I tell them. "I'm so impressed with the ways all of you picked out language that the authors of your books use to link ideas and talked about the importance of that language. Before we finish up today, let's go back to the question I wrote on the board earlier: 'How would the published informational texts be different if you removed the words that link ideas?' What do you all think? How would they be different?"

Students all around the room quickly raise their hands. I first call on a young lady who explains, "They just wouldn't make as much sense. Without words that link ideas, they'd just be like a bunch of facts that aren't connected. My group used the book *If You Lived in Colonial Times* and the book used the word 'another' to connect statements. Without this word, the things in the book wouldn't connect. They'd just be a bunch of facts."

"A great description of the importance of this writing concept," I reply. "Really nice job today, everyone."

Recommendations for Teaching Students about Linking Ideas

In this section, I describe a step-by-step instructional process to use when teaching students about linking ideas in informational writing. The instructional steps I recommend are: 1) Show students published examples of informational texts in which authors link ideas; 2) Talk with students about why linking ideas is important to effective informational writing; 3) Ask students to analyze what published informational texts would be like if their authors did not link ideas; 4) Ask students to analyze what their own informational texts would be like if those texts didn't include language that links ideas; and 5) Help students reflect on the importance of linking ideas to effective informational writing. Each of these recommendations is described in detail in this section.

1. Show students published examples of informational texts in which authors link ideas.

The first step in this instructional process is to show students published examples of informational texts in which authors link ideas; examining how published authors use specific writing concepts provides an authentic understanding of how those concepts are used in practice. When recently talking with a group of fourth graders about the writing concept of link-ing ideas, I explained to them why I was showing them examples of published authors linking the ideas in their works: "I'm showing you these examples because one of the best ways to learn about writing is to see what other writers do and learn from their strategies. When you look at what these published authors do, you can see how they link ideas in their own works and eventually think about ways you might link the ideas in your writing." Approaching a text in this way helps students read from a writer's perspective, which is integral to the mentor-text approach to writing instruction; while there are many things students can notice when reading a published informational text, these students under-stood they were to focus on specific ways these authors link ideas in their works.

2. Talk with students about why linking ideas is important to effective informational writing.

Once you've shown students published examples of authors linking ideas in their works, the next step is to talk with students about why linking ideas is an important component of effective informational writ-ing. This step extends logically from the first one: now that students know what it looks like when authors link ideas, they're ready to think about the importance of this concept. When I talk with students about the importance of linking ideas to informational writing, I emphasize that authors use words and phrases that link ideas such as "also, another, and, because, but, especially, for example, in contrast," and "however" to show the relationship between statements and make the piece easy to read. To illustrate this, I compare an original excerpt from a piece of published informational text with how that excerpt would look without the words or phrases used to link ideas. I've found that showing stu-dents these excerpts allows them to fully grasp the importance of this concept.

For example, when recently working with a fourth-grade class, I showed them the following excerpt from Daniel Gilpin's book, *Snails, Shellfish, & Other Mollusks* (2006) discussed earlier in this chapter: "Slugs and snails are small, slow-moving, silent creatures. Also, they are most active at night, so they are often overlooked" (p. 26) and then showed them how that passage would look without the word "also," which links the ideas in these sentences. To help the students compare these passages, I use a table like the one depicted in Figure 5.3.

Figure 5.3 Excerpt from Published Text With and Without Language that Links Ideas

Title and author of book used	Original excerpt with language that links ideas	Excerpt rewritten without language that links ideas
Snails, Shellfish, & Other Mollusks by Daniel Gilpin	"Slugs and snails are small, slow-moving, silent creatures. <u>Also</u>, they are most active at night, so they are often overlooked." (p. 26)	Slugs and snails are small, slow-moving, silent creatures. They are most active at night, so they are often overlooked.

I read each passage to the students, highlighting the importance of the word "also" to the original text by calling attention to the way it links the ideas in each of these statements and helps the text read as smoothly as possible. Emphasizing the significance of this idea-linking word helps students understand the importance of this writing concept.

3. Ask students to analyze what published informational texts would be like if their authors did not link ideas.

The next step of this instructional process is to engage students in their own analysis of the importance of this concept by asking them what published informational texts would be like if their authors did not link ideas. This activity, an example of which is described in this chapter's classroom snapshot, calls for students to select an informational text, identify an excerpt that uses language to link ideas, rewrite that excerpt without the language that links ideas, and analyze the differences in those excerpts. Before asking your students to engage in this activity, I recommend showing them an example so that they have a clear understanding of what to do. In the lesson described in the classroom snapshot, I showed my students an example that incorporates an excerpt from Anne M. Todd's (2003) book *Sitting Bull*. I talked to my students about the original version of this passage, which uses the word "instead" to link ideas, the revised version without this word, and my analysis of why "instead" is important to the original text. Once students have seen an example like this one and asked any clarifying questions they have about it, they're ready to do the activity. Students can do this activity in groups—as described in the classroom snapshot—or independently. Figure 5.4 depicts a student's work on this activity using the book *Oceans* by Beverly McMillan and John Musick (2007).

Once students have completed these analyses of published works, it's time to move to the next step of this instructional process, in which students analyze their own informational texts.

Figure 5.4 Student Work on Linking Ideas Activity Using Published Work

Title and author of the book you used	Example from text that contains language that links ideas	Example rewritten without language that links ideas	Why you think the language that links ideas is important to the original text
Oceans by Beverly McMillan and John Musick	"Old ships... provide homes for many forms of Ocean life. For example, sea anemones and some Mollusks live only where they can attach to a hard surface and some fish only where they can hide." (p. 24)	"Old ships... provide homes for many forms of ocean life. Sea anemones and some mollusks live only where they can attach to a hard surface, and some fish only where they can hide."	The reason why you would want that key word, for example, is because you wouldn't understand what it would mean. It would cause a mis-conception. It links the ideas of the 2 sentences.

4. Ask students to analyze what their own informational texts would be like if those texts didn't include language that links ideas.

For the fourth step of this instructional process, I recommend asking students to analyze what their own informational writing would look like without language that links ideas. When I do this with students, I first ask them to apply the strategy of linking ideas to their own informational works by using words and phrases such as those we've discussed in their own writing. As students do this, I hold one-on-one conferences with them in which I ask them to show me specific instances in which they've linked ideas in their works. Once the students have applied this strategy to their pieces, I engage them in an activity designed to help them consider what their works would be like without language that links ideas. This activity is similar to the one described in the third step in this instructional process, but also differs in a significant way: it asks students to analyze the importance of idea-linking language to their own works, instead of in those written by published authors. Analyzing

Figure 5.5 Student Work on Linking Ideas Activity using Student's Own Work

Text you created that uses language that links ideas	That text, without the language that links ideas	Why you think the language that links ideas is important to the original text you created
My brother and I have a lot of things in common. We especially love computers and technology.	My brother and I have a lot in common. We love computers and technology.	The word especially is important because it points out specifically what the brothers have most in common. It links the ideas together.

their own works can help students see the significance of the concept of linking ideas to their own writing.

When asking students to do this activity, I give each of them a chart that asks them to do the following: identify a selection from his or her work that uses language that links ideas, rewrite that text without the language that links ideas, and write why he or she believes that language that links ideas is important to the original text. Figure 5.5 contains an example of a student's work on this activity. (A reproducible template of this chart for you to copy and use with your own students is available in the Appendix).

After the students have completed this activity, I like to ask for volunteers to share their examples and analyses with the rest of the class. Sharing these works further illustrates the importance of this concept to effective writing and segues nicely into the final step of this process, in which students reflect on the importance of linking ideas to effective informational writing.

5. Help students reflect on the importance of linking ideas to effective informational writing.

In the final step of this instructional process, since the students have at this point looked at many examples of language that links ideas and considered their significance, I believe that ending this instructional process with a final reflection on the importance of this concept provides a strong sense of closure. In addition, students who reflect on why linking ideas is an important aspect of strong informational writing can enhance their metacognitive awareness of how this concept can be a tool that they can use to enhance their future works. To help students reflect on the importance of this writing strategy, I write the question "Why is it important that informational writers link the ideas in their works?" on the board and ask the students to discuss the question in small groups. After the students talk in their small groups, I ask for volunteers to share their insights with the whole class. When I was recently talking with a fourth-grade class about this topic, I was impressed by a student who shared, "Informational writers need to link their ideas so that the whole book or essay sounds connected and not just like a bunch of things written down that aren't really related. Writers need to show readers how the things they say are related so that readers can get it." This student's awareness of the importance of this concept reveals strong insights into how linking ideas enhances a piece of writing and suggests that she will continue to see it as important tool when composing her future works.

Final Thoughts on Linking Ideas

- ◆ Linking ideas when writing informational text is addressed in Common Core Writing Standards W.3.2c, W.4.2c, and W.5.2c.
- ◆ When linking ideas, authors use words and phrases such as "also, another, and, because, but, especially, for example," and "in contrast" (Common Core State Standards, 2010).
- ◆ Authors link ideas that are similar, as well as those that are different from each other.
- ◆ Linking ideas is important to effective informational writing because doing so communicates the relationship between key ideas and helps make the piece as easy to read as possible.
- ◆ When teaching students about linking ideas:
  - ◆ Show students published examples of informational texts in which authors link ideas.
  - ◆ Talk with students about why linking ideas is important to effective informational writing.
  - ◆ Ask students to analyze what published informational texts would be like if their authors did not link ideas.
  - ◆ Ask students to analyze what their own informational texts would be like if those texts didn't include language that links ideas.
  - ◆ Help students reflect on the importance of linking ideas to effective informational writing.

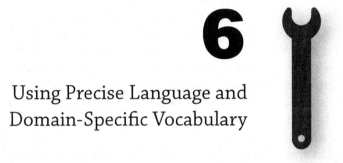

6

Using Precise Language and Domain-Specific Vocabulary

What Does "Using Precise Language and Domain-Specific Vocabulary" Mean?

An important tool for effective informational writing is the use of precise language and domain-specific vocabulary when describing particular topics. As we'll discuss in this chapter, precise language and domain-specific vocabulary provide information that can maximize a reader's understanding of a text. Common Core Writing Standards W.4.2d and W.5.2d highlight the significance of this concept, emphasizing that writers "Use precise language and domain-specific vocabulary to inform about or explain the topic" (Common Core State Standards, 2010). In this chapter, we'll discuss the following: what "using precise language and domain-specific vocabulary" means, why it is important for effective informational writing, a description of a lesson on this concept, and key recommendations for helping your students use precise language and domain-specific vocabulary in their own informational writing.

We'll start by considering what it means to use precise language and domain-specific vocabulary. In the context of informational writing, "precise language and domain-specific vocabulary" refers to language that clearly represents what an author is trying to describe and is related to a particular subject area and topic. Since informational writers address specialized topics in their works, such as scientific phenomena, significant events, and historical figures, they often use terms specific to those topics to make their works as clear as possible. If an author is describing particular muscles in the human body, she would want to use vocabulary terms specific to this area of study to maximize the clarity of her work. For example, using the term "biceps" would be much more specific than saying "muscles in the arm." By using this specific term, the author can ensure the reader knows exactly which arm muscles she is describing, which makes her writing as informative as possible.

To further illustrate this concept, let's take a look at a published example in which an author uses precise language and domain-specific vocabulary to clearly describe a topic. In Marilyn Singer's (2007) informational book *Venom*, she uses precise language and domain-specific vocabulary in the sentence, "The proteins in various toxins—often in the form of enzymes—attack cells and tissues, disrupt communication between nerve endings, and cause other damage" (p. 6). This sentence contains precise and domain-specific terms such as "proteins," "toxins" and "enzymes" to accurately capture the information Singer wants the reader to take from this passage. Singer's use of these terms adds specificity and clarity to this passage. In addition, she uses other examples of concrete language, such as "cells" and tissues," to indicate to readers exactly what is being attacked.

Why Using Precise Language and Domain-Specific Vocabulary Is Important to Effective Writing

The use of precise language and domain-specific vocabulary is important to effective informational writing because it makes an author's work as clear and specific as possible. Without the use of precise and specific terminology, informational writing would be vague, general, and not especially informative. A book about a particular scientific phenomenon without precise language and domain-specific vocabulary wouldn't provide much information about that topic because of the lack of specific and concrete language used. For example, a description of the water cycle would be difficult to understand without terms such as "evaporation" and "precipitation." With these terms, however, an author can describe the water cycle with clarity and specificity.

It's also important to note that precise language and domain-specific vocabulary allows writers to express important ideas concisely. Without precise and specific terms, authors would need to rely on excessively wordy explanations to convey an idea that could be expressed through a particular word. Imagine reading a book about space travel in which the author never used the word "astronaut" and described what an astronaut is each time instead. This would make reading the piece more time consuming than necessary because the author would be using wordy descriptions in place of a specific term. In this section, we'll examine the importance of precise language and domain-specific vocabulary by looking at some published examples of these concepts and reflecting on how these examples would read if the precise language and specific vocabulary were replaced by vague and general language.

First, let's take a look at the language and vocabulary used in the following passage from Miranda Macquitty's informational book *Shark* (2004): "To breathe, sharks have gills that absorb oxygen from the water and release carbon dioxide back into it" (p. 10). In this sentence, Macquitty uses domain-specific language such as "gills" and precise terms such as "oxygen" and "carbon dioxide." Without these words, this passage would not be as informative or concise; replacing them with less specific and precise language could produce the following passage: "To breathe, sharks have *body parts* that absorb *some things* from the water and release *other things* back into it." This revised version does not have the specificity of Macquitty's original text; it provides far less information and uses more words than the original passage. As this comparison illustrates, the use of precise language and domain-specific vocabulary makes a significant difference in the quality of an informational passage. Figure 6.1 contains the original passage from *Shark*, as well as the revised example without the precise language and domain-specific vocabulary.

Another informational text that effectively uses precise language and domain-specific vocabulary is Daniel Gilpin's book *Starfish, Urchins, & Other Echinoderms* (2006). These terms are especially evident in the following passage about starfish: "Starfish have incredible powers of regeneration. If they lose a limb to a predator, they soon grown another one" (p. 13). This passage incorporates examples of precise language and domain-specific vocabulary such as "limb" and "predator" and "regeneration." Gilpin's use of these terms allows for this excerpt to be as clear and informative as possible. Rewritten without these examples of precise language and domain-specific vocabulary, the passage could read, "Starfish have incredible powers of *regrowing a lost body part*. If they lose a *body part* to *an animal that kills and eats others*, they soon grow another one." Let's consider the differences in these two passages. While Gilpin's original version uses the specific term "regeneration," the second example replaces that word with the phrase "regrowing a lost body part." Not only is this replacement wordier, but it also doesn't convey the same scientific tone that the original text has. In addition, the original text uses the words "limb" and "predator," which appear as "body part" and "an animal that

Figure 6.1 Original and Revised Examples from *Shark*

Original Text	Text Without Precise Language and Domain-Specific Vocabulary
"To breathe, sharks have <u>gills</u> that absorb <u>oxygen</u> from the water and release <u>carbon dioxide</u> back into it." (p. 10)	"To breathe, sharks have <u>body parts</u> that absorb <u>some things</u> from the water and release <u>other things</u> back into it."

Figure 6.2 Original and Revised Examples from *Starfish, Urchins, & Other Echinoderms*

Original Text	Text Without Precise Language and Domain-Specific Vocabulary
"Starfish have incredible powers of regeneration. If they lose a limb to a predator, they soon grown another one." (p. 13)	"Starfish have incredible powers of regrowing a lost body part. If they lose a body part to an animal that kills and eats others, they soon grow another one."

kills and eats others" in the second passage. "Limb" is more specific and concise than "body part," as it uses fewer words to give readers a clearer picture of what is being described, and "predator" conveys its intended meaning much more directly than "an animal that kills and eats others." Gilpin's informative and clear passage is made possible in large part by the specific and precise terms he uses. Without these terms, the passage would be far less effective. Figure 6.2 pairs the original passage from *Starfish, Urchins, & Other Echinoderms* with the revised one.

As these discussions of passages from *Shark* and *Starfish, Urchins, & Other Echinoderms* illustrate, the use of precise language and domain-specific vocabulary is a key component of effective informational writing. Without the precise and specific terms discussed in these sections, these passages would be unclear and wordy. With them, however, these excerpts provide important information in clear and concise language. In the next section, we'll take a look inside a fifth-grade classroom and see the students in this class work on this important writing concept.

A Classroom Snapshot

Today is my third day working with a class of wonderful fifth graders on the writing skill of using precise language and domain-specific vocabulary while writing informational texts. In our first meeting, we discussed what precise language and domain-specific vocabulary is, and I showed the students a number of published informational texts that feature these kinds of terms. When we met for the second time, the students and I talked about the importance of informational authors using precise language and domain-specific vocabulary in their works. I explained that these terms are useful tools for effective informational writing because they enable writers to provide information in a clear and specific way, and to do so without using excess language. Now that the students have developed a solid knowledge base about the use of precise language and domain-specific vocabulary, it's time to allow them more responsibility in their work with this concept.

I begin today's class with an out-of-school connection: "I was thinking about precise language and domain-specific vocabulary yesterday when

I was at a baseball game with my children." Some of the students smile amusedly, so I jokingly add, "Yes, I think about this stuff all the time." Returning to my original train of thought, I explain, "My children and I were talking about pitching, and I told one of my children, 'The pitcher threw a curveball to the batter.' Right after I said this, I started thinking, 'What would that statement have been like without any precise language and domain-specific vocabulary?' So, I'd like to ask you all to think about this, too."

I write on the whiteboard, "The pitcher threw a curveball to the bat-ter," and then tell the students, "What we're going to do, to get started with today's work, is to think about how this sentence would look without precise language and domain-specific vocabulary. In order to do that, we need to first figure out where the precise language and domain-specific vocabulary is in this sentence. I'll get us started by identifying one exam-ple." I underline the word "pitcher" in the sentence and explain, "The word 'pitcher' is an example of precise language and domain-specific vocabulary. It's a baseball term for a player who throws the ball to another team's batter, and it lets us know which player is being described. Can anyone tell us a less specific and precise way to refer to a pitcher?"

One student raises her hand and shares, "The player throwing the ball."

"Very good," I reply. "Saying 'the player throwing the ball' is definitely a less specific and precise way to refer to a pitcher. It doesn't use the domain-specific baseball term and it's wordier. Who can find another example of precise and domain-specific language in this sentence?"

Another student raises his hand and says, "'The 'batter' is another one."

"Nice job," I respond. "Like 'pitcher,' 'batter' is a baseball term for a player—in this case, the player who is holding a bat and swinging at the ball thrown by the pitcher. What's a less specific and precise way to say this?"

The student answers, "You could say, 'the one swinging the bat.'"

"Good," I praise the student. "We can compare this to our classmate's statement that we can turn 'pitcher' to 'the player throwing the ball.' Similarly, we can turn 'batter' into 'the one swinging the bat.' That is definitely a less domain-specific way to say 'batter.' Now, can anyone find any other examples of precise language and domain-specific vocabulary in this sentence?"

After a brief pause, a few student hands go into the air. I call on a student who explains, "I think 'curveball' is one."

"Excellent," I reply. "'Curveball is a specific baseball term that refers to a kind of pitch. Can you think of a less specific way to say 'curveball'?'"

"'A ball,' or 'a pitch'" responds this student.

"So," I follow up, "instead of saying, 'The pitcher threw a curveball to the batter,' I could have said to my children, 'The player throwing the ball threw a pitch to the one swinging the bat.'" I write the new version of this sentence on the whiteboard next to the original one to clearly illustrate the differences. "Why would someone use the original version of this sentence, which contains precise language and domain-specific vocabulary, instead of the second one?"

I call on a young lady who explains, "The first one just makes a lot more sense. It's definitely clearer what the sentence is talking about and it's not as long."

"Great job," I respond. "Today, we're going to work in groups and do an activity that resembles what we just did as a class, except that I'm not going to be giving you the sentences. You'll find examples from published informational texts that use precise language and domain-specific vocabulary, replace some of the specific terms in them with less specific ones, and then analyze why the specific language and vocabulary are important to the original examples. I don't want you to start yet, though. First, I want to show you an example."

I place on the document camera the chart depicted in Figure 6.3 and tell the students, "Here is an example of the kind of product you'll have after you finish this activity."

"As you can see, I identified a line from this book that contains domain-specific vocabulary, underlined those specific terms, rewrote that line with those terms replaced with less specific ones, and then commented on why I think the specific vocabulary is important to the original text."

I then explain to the students that they'll be doing this activity in the small groups in which they're seated. I give each group a blank copy of the chart depicted in Figure 6.3 (a reproducible version of this chart that you can copy and use in your classroom is available in the Appendix) and instruct them to select an informational text from the classroom library to use for this activity. "Remember to pick an example from your book that uses precise and domain-specific language," I tell them. "Once you do that, you can replace those specific terms with general ones and analyze them. I'll come around and check in with all of the groups. Good luck!"

The students select informational texts from the classroom library and examine them with their group members, discussing precise and domain-specific language in those works. Once it seems like the students have made some progress in this activity, I begin checking in with the small groups. I first talk with a group that is working with an informational work called *The Book of Eagles* (Sattler, 1989). As I pull up a chair and sit down with the students, one of them quickly says, "Look at this sentence we found. It uses a lot of domain-specific vocabulary."

"Wonderful," I respond.

"Yeah," continues the student. "It's about biologists tracking eagles to learn more about them. The sentence is, 'Others strap transmitters to the backs of fledglings and track them with satellites,'" she explains, pointing to page 30 of the book.

Figure 6.3 Example of Specific Vocabulary in Published Text Analysis Chart

Title and author of the book you used	Line from text containing domain-specific vocabulary	Line from text with domain-specific vocabulary replaced by more general language	Why you think the domain-specific vocabulary is important to the original text
The Tarantula Scientist by Sy Montgomery	"<u>Chilean tarantula</u> venom might help <u>heart attack victims</u>." (p. 75)	"<u>Some spiders'</u> venom might help <u>people with certain health problems</u>."	The domain-specific terms "Chilean tarantula" and "heart attack victims" make the original sentence much clearer than the revised version. The second sentence doesn't give much specific information at all. In that one, we don't know what spiders are being discussed or what the health problems are. The original sentence is also more concise than the revised one.

"A really good sentence," I reply. "What domain-specific vocabulary did you notice?"

"We picked out three!" exclaims another student in the group. "They are 'transmitters,' 'fledglings,' and 'satellites.' We replaced transmitters with 'technological devices,' we changed 'fledglings' to 'baby eagles,' and we replaced 'satellites' with 'other technological devices.' Our new sentence became, 'Others strap technological devices to baby eagles and track them with other technological devices.'"

"Very nice job," I tell the group. "How about your analysis? Why do you think the domain-specific vocabulary is important to the original version?"

"It's a lot more specific with the domain-specific vocabulary," explains the student. "Plus, the sentence doesn't use as many words. When we changed 'transmitters' and 'satellites' to 'technological devices,' that made the sentence worse because you wouldn't know what technological devices the author's talking about. When we changed 'fledglings' to 'baby eagles,' that made the sentence so that it needed more words to say the same thing. The domain-specific vocabulary definitely makes the sentence better."

Thrilled with the group's response and analysis, I praise their work and check in with the other groups. Another group has selected the following sentence from page 10 of Peter Riley's book *Food Chains* (1998), "Omnivores may search in many places for their food," and changed the domain-specific term "omnivores" to the much more general "some animals," creating the new sentence, "Some animals may search in many places for their food." A student in the group explained the importance of domain-specific vocabulary to the original sentence by saying, "The word 'omnivores' is really important to the original sentence because it tells you exactly what kind of animals the sentence is about. 'Some animals' doesn't tell you what kind of animals the sentence is about, but 'omnivores' does."

After checking in with the other small groups in the class—and being similarly impressed by their equally strong work—I praise the class' performance: "Fantastic job on this activity. I love the way all of you found precise and domain-specific language in your books, changed them to general examples, and analyzed the differences. You're really understanding this! I can't wait to see you apply this strategy to your own writing!"

Recommendations for Teaching Students about Using Precise Language and Domain-Specific Vocabulary

In this section, I describe a step-by-step instructional process to use when teaching students about using precise language and domain-specific vocabulary in informational writing. The instructional steps I recommend are: 1) Show students examples of precise language and domain-specific vocabulary used in published informational texts; 2) Talk with students about how precise language and domain-specific vocabulary are important to effective informational writing; 3) Have students analyze the importance of precise language and domain-specific vocabulary in published works; 4) Have students analyze the importance of precise language and domain-specific vocabulary in their own works; and 5) Ask students to reflect on why precise language and domain-specific vocabulary are important tools for effective writing. Each of these recommendations is described in detail in this section.

1. Show students examples of precise language and domain-specific vocabulary used in published informational texts.

I recommend beginning this instructional process by showing students examples of precise language and domain-specific vocabulary used in published informational texts. When showing these kinds of examples to my students, I like to bring in a wide range of informational works addressing a number of subjects. For example, I recently conducted this activity with a group of fifth graders and wanted to be sure that they understood the many ways informational authors incorporate precise and specific terms into their works. Since many of the students in the class said they enjoyed soccer, I began with an article by *Sports Illustrated's* Grant Wahl on soccer's 2014 World Cup, identifying terms like "corner kick" (Wahl, 2014, p. 39) and "hand ball" (p. 42) that are specific to that sport. After beginning with these examples, I transitioned to informational texts about scientific and historical topics that are more typically used in school settings, showing students examples of precise language and domain-specific vocabulary in these works. After seeing such a wide range of specific vocabulary terms, the students developed a strong awareness of what it means to use to precise language and domain-specific vocabulary. In addition, showing students examples of domain-specific terms that relate to subjects they are interested in increases students' engagement by making the lesson relevant to their out-of-school lives (Ladson-Billings, 1995).

2. Talk with students about how precise language and domain-specific vocabulary are important to effective informational writing.

After showing students examples of precise language and domain-specific vocabulary, the next step in this instructional process is to talk with them about why these kinds of terms are important to effective informational writing. When I talk with my students about this topic, I emphasize that the use of precise and specific language is important for two key reasons: 1) It makes an author's work as clear and specific as possible; and 2) It allows writers to express their ideas concisely. To illustrate this, I show students Figures 6.1 and 6.2 from this chapter, which contain excerpts from original versions of informational text and revised versions of those excerpts that do not include precise language and domain-specific vocabulary. While displaying these figures on the document camera, I think aloud about the differences between them, calling attention to the importance of the precise language and domain-specific vocabulary in each example. For example, when showing the students Figure 6.1, which contains the following passage from Miranda Macquitty's informational book *Shark* (2004): "To breathe, sharks have *gills* that absorb *oxygen* from the water and release *carbon dioxide* back into it" (p. 10), I call attention to the specificity that the terms "gills," "oxygen," and "carbon dioxide" provide and compare this passage to the revised example, which reads "To breathe, sharks have *body parts* that absorb *some things* from the water and release *other things* back into it."

When thinking aloud about the differences in these passages, I'll say, "When I read these two sentences, I can really see the importance of using precise language and domain-specific vocabulary. The first sentence is so specific—it tells me what parts of their bodies sharks use to breathe and clearly states what they absorb from the water and what they release back into it. The second sentence doesn't tell me any of that! It's so vague and general. Plus, I notice that the second sentence is actually longer—it uses more words to give us less information! Comparing these sentences really shows me that precise language and domain-specific vocabulary is important to effective informational writing!" By thinking these ideas aloud to my students, I help them understand how the precise language and domain-specific vocabulary used in the original sentence improves my experience reading it, emphasizing the importance of this writing strategy.

3. Have students analyze the importance of precise language and domain-specific vocabulary in published works.

The next step in this instructional process is to have students work on their own or in small groups to analyze the importance of precise language and domain-specific vocabulary in published works. This activity follows the gradual release of responsibility method of instruction, as it calls for students to take more control of their own learning by applying what they've learned in the first two steps of the process. To complete this activity, students need to do the following: 1) Select an informational text; 2) Identify a specific line from that text that features domain-specific vocabulary; 3) Rewrite that line with the domain-specific vocabulary replaced by more general language; and 4) Explain why the domain-specific vocabulary is important to the original text. As students follow these steps, they increase their ability to identify domain-specific vocabulary, as well as their understanding of the importance of this writing tool.

An example of a fifth-grade class working on this activity is described in this chapter's classroom snapshot. As discussed in the snapshot, I like to model this activity for students before asking them to work on it. Once I've shown the students a model of how a completed version of this activity could look and discussed it with them, I turn the students loose and have them work either in small groups or individually on the assignment. While the students work, I sit down with them, check on their progress, and see if they need any support. An example of a student's work on this activity is depicted in Figure 6.4.

4. Have students analyze the importance of precise language and domain-specific vocabulary in their own works.

Figure 6.4 Student Work Analyzing Domain-Specific Vocabulary in Published Text

Title and author of the book you used	Line from text containing domain-specific vocabulary	Line from text with domain-specific vocabulary replaced by more general language	Why you think the domain-specific vocabulary is important to the original text
Volcanoes: Witness to Disaster by Judy and Dennis Fraden	"By April as magma and gas built up intense pressure inside, the mountain had begun to bulge." p.27	"By April as things in the mountain built up intense pressure inside the mountain had begun to bulge"	The sentence with specific vocabulary tells you exactly what built up inside the mountain.

Now that the students have analyzed the importance of precise language and domain-specific vocabulary in published texts, the next step of this instructional process is to ask them to apply this analytical framework to their own works. This step further increases the responsibility placed on the students; they must first create a piece of informational writing that uses domain-specific vocabulary, then select an example and analyze it. When I do this with my students, I first give them some time to create an informational work. While they are working on these pieces, I remind them what precise language and domain-specific vocabulary are and emphasize the importance of including them in informational writing. Once the students have taken some time to work on their pieces, I ask each of them to select a line from their own works that contains domain-specific vocabulary. While students are selecting these lines, I confer with them to be sure that the lines they're selecting do in fact contain domain-specific vocabulary.

After the students have selected these lines, I give each of them a chart that asks them to do the following: 1) Select a sentence the student created that uses domain-specific vocabulary; 2) Rewrite that sentence with the domain-specific vocabulary replaced by more general language; and 3) Analyze why the domain-specific vocabulary is important to the original sentence. Figure 6.5 contains a student's work on this activity

Figure 6.5 Student Work Analyzing Domain-Specific Vocabulary in Student's Own Work

Sentence you created that uses domain-specific vocabulary	That sentence, with the domain-specific vocabulary replaced by more general language	Why you think the domain-specific vocabulary is important to the original sentence you created
When the volcano erupted it caused huge amounts of molten lava to fly out of it.	When the volcano blew up it caused hot things to fly out.	It gives more details and a more exact picture of what is happening.

(a blank, reproducible version of this chart that you can copy and use in your classroom is available in the Appendix).

This student did a nice job of explaining that the domain-specific vocabulary in her original example "gives more details and a more exact picture of what is happening." This analysis shows a strong awareness of the difference between domain-specific language like "molten lava" and more general descriptions such as "hot things."

5. Ask students to reflect on why precise language and domain-specific vocabulary are important tools for effective writing.

The final step in this instructional process is to encourage students to think metacognitively about the use of precise language and domain-specific vocabulary by reflecting on the importance of these concepts to effective writing. Asking students to reflect on why these language forms are useful tools for strong informational writing provides a strong sense of closure to this process and requires students to further consider why informational writers use them in their works. To facilitate this reflection, I place the following text on the document camera or the whiteboard:

Now that you've identified and analyzed precise language and domain-specific vocabulary in published works and in your own writing, think about this question: why do you think the use of precise language and domain-specific vocabulary is an important tool for effective informational writing?

I like for the students to first discuss their thoughts about this question with partners or small group members. Once they've done this, I ask for volunteers to share their thoughts with the rest of the class. During my recent work with a fifth-grade class, one student explained, "They are tools for good informational writing because they're things writers use to make sure readers understand. If you didn't use precise language and specific vocabulary, people might not know what you're saying. Like, you might say 'a group of stars' instead of 'Orion.' If you said 'a group of stars,' people wouldn't know what stars you're talking about. If you said 'Orion,' they'd know you're talking about that constellation." This student, who wrote his informational piece about constellations, did a very nice job of describing the importance of domain-specific vocabulary and precise language to effective informational writing and used a strong example to illustrate his point.

Final Thoughts on Using Precise Language and Domain-Specific Vocabulary

- ◆ Using precise language and domain-specific vocabulary when writing informational text is addressed in Common Core Writing Standards W.4.2d and W.5.2d, which call for writers to "Use precise language and domain-specific vocabulary to inform about or explain the topic" (Common Core State Standards, 2010).
- ◆ In the context of informational writing, "precise language and domain-specific vocabulary" refers to language that clearly represents what an author is trying to describe and is related to a particular subject area and topic.
- ◆ Since informational writers address specialized topics in their works, such as scientific phenomena, significant events, and historical figures, they often use terms specific to those topics to make their works as clear as possible.
- ◆ The use of precise language and domain-specific vocabulary is important to effective informational writing for the following reasons:
  - ◆ It makes an author's work as clear and specific as possible.
  - ◆ It allows writers to express their ideas concisely.
- ◆ When teaching students about precise language and domain-specific vocabulary:
  - ◆ Show students examples of precise language and domain-specific vocabulary used in published informational texts.

- Talk with students about how precise language and domain-specific vocabulary are important to effective informational writing.
- Have students analyze the importance of precise language and domain-specific vocabulary in published works.
- Ask students to reflect on why precise language and domain-specific vocabulary are important tools for effective writing.

Section **2**

Putting It Together

7

Crafting a Concluding Section

What Does "Crafting a Concluding Section" Mean?

In addition to incorporating the elements of effective informational writing described so far in this book, a strong informational text needs to contain a well-written conclusion. The Common Core Writing Standards call for students to craft effective conclusions in their works, as Standards W.3.2d., W.4.2e, and W.5.2e discuss the importance of this concept. In this chapter, we'll discuss the following: what "crafting a concluding section" means, why this concept is important to effective informational writing, a description of a lesson on this concept, and key recommendations for helping your students craft strong concluding sections in their own works.

First, let's think about what it means to craft a concluding section. A concluding section of an informational text is a closing statement of one or more paragraphs that provides a sense of closure to the piece. William Zinsser, in his book *On Writing Well* (2006), explains that a conclusion should not simply be a summary of information already presented in the piece. A conclusion that only summarizes previously stated points usually bores readers, Zinsser explains, and doesn't enhance the quality of the piece. While it's true that a conclusion should, as the Common Core Standards explain, be "related to the information or explanation presented" in the piece, it should not be a summary paragraph of what's already been said. Instead, an especially effective conclusion should do two things: 1) Highlight the significance of the piece's topic; and 2) Leave readers with a final thought or message about this topic.

To illustrate these components of an effective conclusion, let's take a look at an example from Jeanette Larson and Adrienne Yorinks' (2011) informational text *Hummingbirds*, which highlights the significance of the

Figure 7.1 How *Hummingbirds* Performs the Key Actions of a Conclusion

Action Performed by Conclusion	Excerpt from *Hummingbirds* that Performs this Action
1. Highlight the significance of the piece's topic.	"Hummingbirds have been objects of fascination for centuries . . . the existence of hummingbirds is documented in pre-Columbian artifacts and artwork."
2. Leave readers with a final thought or message about this topic.	"Though tenacious, hummingbirds are still small birds, dependent on the environment for their survival. We need to be vigilant so that hundreds of years from now, when other children are studying hummingbirds, they will still be able to see these remarkable creatures with their own eyes."

topic and leaves readers with an important message. This book's concluding section begins with the statement, "Hummingbirds have been objects of fascination for centuries . . . the existence of hummingbirds is documented in pre-Columbian artifacts and artwork" (p. 54) and concludes with the following thought:

> Though tenacious, hummingbirds are still small birds, dependent on the environment for their survival. We need to be vigilant so that hundreds of years from now, when other children are studying hummingbirds, they will still be able to see these remarkable creatures with their own eyes. (p. 54)

In this conclusion, Larson and Yorinks highlight the significance of hummingbirds by describing a long-held fascination with them. In addition, they leave readers with some final thoughts on this topic by first explaining that hummingbirds depend on the environment and then calling on today's people to take care of the environment in general, and hummingbirds in particular, so that future generations can also enjoy them. Figure 7.1 uses a chart to depict the important actions of a conclusion and the excerpts from Larson and Yorinks' text that perform them.

Why Crafting a Concluding Section Is Important to Effective Writing

A strong conclusion is an important tool for creating an effective piece of informational writing. Without a conclusion, a piece of writing would lack any sense of closure. An informational piece with no closure could be frustrating and confusing to readers, who expected the author to provide some final thoughts on the topic that the piece is addressing. However, as stated in the previous section, a well-crafted conclusion will not simply be a summary of previously made points; instead, it will highlight the significance of the topic and leave readers with a final thought or message. Let's think about why each one of these components is especially important to an effective conclusion.

Highlight the Significance of a Topic

Highlighting the significance of a topic is an important aspect of an effective conclusion because it emphasizes the value of the work to the reader. No one wants to finish reading a text and think, "I don't know why I just spent time reading about that topic." Instead, readers want to finish a piece and think, "That was a really interesting topic and I learned a lot of important information about it!" By highlighting the significance of a topic, informational authors help their readers achieve the latter response. When working with my students on this concept, I tell them that this part of the conclusion is where authors remind their readers that the topic of their work is important. There are a variety of ways to do this, and these ways are often specific to the particular topic, but I make sure my students understand that they should highlight the importance of the topic when crafting a conclusion.

Leave Readers with a Final Thought or Message

It is also important that a conclusion leaves readers with a final thought or message related to the piece's topic, as doing so gives readers something to continue to think about once they've finished reading the work. William Zinsser (2006) explains that a strong conclusion "gives the reader a lift, and it lingers when the article is over" (p. 65). Applied specifically to elementary school informational writing, Zinsser's comment illustrates that our students' works should continue to stay with their readers once those readers have finished. Leaving readers with a final thought or message about the piece's topic allows this to occur.

Now, let's take a look at the conclusion from a published informational text and examine why this conclusion is important to the success of the piece. In Mary Barrett Brown's (1992) informational text, *Wings along the Waterway*, the author uses the conclusion to highlight the significance of water birds and leave readers with a final message that stays with them after they've concluded the piece:

> Although water birds are resourceful, they need our attention to survive. Civilization may be their greatest threat. Encroachment upon the wetlands, and drainage of the birds' habitat can quickly reduce their population. Pollution and pesticides also threaten their survival. And so we observe them and learn, and in the

process we discover the sense of wonder these birds and their special world can inspire. As long as the waterways last, there will be water birds. (p. 77)

In this concluding paragraph, Brown asserts that water birds are special and urges readers to think about their preservation. She calls attention to the special nature of water birds by calling them "resourceful" and stating that, as we observe and learn about them, "we discover the sense of wonder these birds and their special world can inspire." These statements address the importance of this topic and suggest that the reader has just spent time reading about some special and wonderful birds! In addition, Brown does an excellent job in this section of leaving readers with a final thought and message about the importance of preserving water birds. She calls civilization water birds' "greatest threat" and identifies ways that the birds' survival is threatened. Brown's final sentences—"As long as the waterways last, there will be water birds"—urges readers to ensure that waterways stay intact, as this will allow water birds to continue to exist. This is a powerful final message with which to leave the reader. If Mary Barrett Brown did not conclude her book with this final section, she wouldn't leave readers with such important thoughts. Note that Brown does not summarize a great deal of information here; instead, she creates a well-crafted conclusion that highlights the special nature of water birds and leaves us with an important message about preserving water birds and waterways.

Another especially effective conclusion is found in Dorothy Hinshaw Patent's book, *Horses of America* (1981). Patent concludes this book by highlighting the significance of horses to American history and culture and states that horses will continue to figure prominently in people's lives:

Horses have always been important in our country. They helped people explore and settle the land. They still work on farms and ranches. And they help people enjoy life by providing exciting competition, pleasant riding, and loving friendship. Because of their strength, loyalty, and beauty, horses will continue to play important roles in human life. (p. 76)

Patent's concluding paragraph clearly and effectively fulfills the key roles of a conclusion by emphasizing the importance of the book's topic and leaving readers with an important final thought. Like Mary Barrett Brown's conclusion to her book about water birds, Patent does not use the conclusion to summarize a great deal of information about horses—the conclusion doesn't, for example, recap the attributes and distinguishing characteristics of the many horses described in the book. Instead, the conclusion to *Horses of America* emphasizes key ways that horses have been important to life in the United States, such as assisting settlers, working on farms, and providing enjoyment and companionship. After highlighting these ways that horses in American have been significant, Patent leaves the reader with the final thought that "horses will continue play important roles in human life."

As Brown's and Patent's conclusions illustrate, an effective conclusion is important to a well-crafted piece of informational writing. Conclusions provide a sense of closure to a piece of writing, and an especially effective conclusion will highlight the significance of a topic and leave readers with an important final thought or message that will stay with them after they've finished reading. In the next section, we'll take a look inside a fifth-grade classroom and see how the students in that class explored the writing tool of crafting an effective conclusion.

A Classroom Snapshot

"You all did such a great job yesterday," I say as I open today's lesson with my fifth graders on crafting effective conclusions, "so I really can't wait to see how you apply that knowledge today!"

The students smile, seeming to appreciate the praise. Before continuing further into today's lesson, I ask the students, "Can someone recap what we talked about yesterday?"

A number of hands fly into the air; I call on a young lady who explains, "[We talked about] why conclusions are important. You said that authors use conclusions to wrap up the things they're writing."

"Great," I respond. "Can anyone tell us the two things that good conclusions do?"

Again, many of the fifth graders raise their hands. I call on another student who states, "They should highlight why the subject is important and give readers a final thing to think about."

"Very nice job," I say. "Conclusions should highlight the significance of the topic and leave readers with a final thought or message about that topic. Today, we're going to think more about how published conclusions do this, but you'll be doing most of the work!" I tell the students with a smile. "Remember how last time I showed you some published examples of conclusions and we talked about how the authors of those conclusions highlight the importance of their subjects and leave readers with a final thought or message?" Several students reply "Yeah," while others nod their heads.

"Well," I continue, "today I'm going to ask you to work in your small groups and do the same thing. You and your group members will pick an informational book from the classroom library, find its conclusion, and identify a part of the conclusion that highlights the significance of the topic as well as a part of the conclusion that leaves the reader with a final thought or message. I'll give each group a chart to fill out while you work."

I place the chart depicted in Figure 7.2 on the document camera (a reproducible version of this chart that you can copy and use in your own classroom is available in the Appendix) and tell the students, "Here's the chart that you and your group members will fill out. You'll pick a book and write down an excerpt from the book that performs each of the key actions of a conclusion. You'll use the same book for both actions."

"Before you start," I tell the students, "I'm going to show you a model of what a completed version of this chart could look like. This example uses one of the books we talked about yesterday—*Horses of America* by Dorothy Hinshaw Patent. Let's take a look." I place the chart depicted in Figure 7.3 on the document camera.

"When I created this chart," I explain, "I looked at the conclusion of this book for an excerpt that highlights the significance of horses, and then for another excerpt that leaves readers with a final thought or message about horses. Every conclusion is different; in this one, the first four sentences of the paragraph highlight the significance of horses, and the last sentence leaves us with a final thought about how horses will continue

Figure 7.2 Template: How a Published Book Performs the Key Actions of a Conclusion

Action Performed by Conclusion	Book You Used	Excerpt from the Book that Performs this Action
1. Highlight the significance of the piece's topic.		
2. Leave readers with a final thought or message about this topic.		

Figure 7.3 Example: How a Published Book Performs the Key Actions of a Conclusion

Action Performed by Conclusion	Book You Used	Excerpt from the Book that Performs this Action
1. Highlight the significance of the piece's topic.	*Horses of America* by Dorothy Hinshaw Patent	"Horses have always been important in our country. They helped people explore and settle the land. They still work on farms and ranches. And they help people enjoy life by providing exciting competition, pleasant riding, and loving friendship." (p.76)

to be important to people. I'll leave this up here while you work, so you can see it and use it as an example to help guide you. Now I'm going to give each of you a chart to fill out with an informational text that you and your group members choose. Just let me know if you have any questions while you're working."

I give each group the template depicted in Figure 7.2 and circulate around the room as the students begin working. I listen carefully as each group selects its book, turns to the conclusion, and identifies excerpts from the book's conclusion that highlight the significance of the book's topic, as well as others that leave readers with a final thought or message about the topic. I'm impressed by how well the students are analyzing the conclusions and determining how the conclusions are highlighting the significance of a particular book's topic while also leaving the reader with a final thought.

Once it seems like the students have made progress with this activity, I begin to confer with the different groups. I begin by sitting down next to a group that is working with a book called *Neandertals: A Prehistoric Puzzle* by Yvette La Pierre (2008). "How's it going?" I ask. "What do you think about your book's conclusion?"

"This book is very cool!" gushes one student in the group. "It's all about prehistoric people."

"Yeah," interjects another student. "There's a whole lot of information here. I really didn't know people knew so much about this."

"The conclusion has a lot of information, too," states another student in the group, "but we think we've found parts that highlight the importance of the topic and parts that leave readers with a final thought."

"Great!" I respond. "What did you find?"

"For the part that highlights the importance of the topic, we picked out this section" (the student reads aloud from page 101 of the text):

As our closest relatives and the last human species we shared the world with, we will always be fascinated with Neandertals. And perhaps it's human nature to be most interested in comparing them to us, to use Neandertals to better understand ourselves. So researchers will continue to look for clues to who the Neandertals were, how they lived, and why they disappeared.

"Good job," I tell the group. "Tell me, why do you see this part as highlighting the importance of the topic?"

"Because it tells about how we will always be fascinated with Neandertals and will want to compare them to ourselves. That means Neandertals are important to people," responds one student.

"And," interjects another student in the group, "it says that researchers will continue to look for clues about them. That also shows they're important."

"Nice job," I respond. "You did a really good job there of identifying how the author highlights the importance of Neandertals. Now, what final thoughts does the author leave us with in this conclusion?"

One student in the group explains, "The author says" (reading aloud from the text):

And we'll continue to wonder about how human they were. Were they curious about the world and their place in it? Did they tell stories about the past? Did they dream about the future? Did they think and feel as we do? That's something the bones will never be able to tell us. (p. 101)

I ask the group how this excerpt reveals final thoughts with which the author wants to leave us, and a student states, "These questions give us something to wonder about. The author wants us to keep wondering about these things after we finish the conclusion."

"Wonderful insight," I exclaim. "Sometimes writers will use questions in their conclusions for the reason you just identified—to keep us wondering about certain ideas after we're done reading. By asking these questions about Neandertals, this author definitely leaves us with some final ideas and wonderings about the possible similarities between humans and Neandertals. Awesome job, you all!"

Next, I sit down with a group that is working with the book *The Life and Times of the Ant* by Charles Micucci (2003). "Hi everyone," I greet them, "let's talk about the conclusion to *The Life and Times of the Ant.*"

"Okay," responds one student. "Here's the part that shows that ants are important. It shows they're important because they've survived for so long." Reading aloud from page 30 of the text, she says:

Ants evolved from wasps more than 100 million years ago. They have been dodging footsteps ever since. As dinosaurs thundered above ground, ants dug out a home below. The mighty dinosaurs are long gone, but the little ant has survived.

"Good job picking that out," I tell the student, "and I love that, before you even read it, you explained how this passage highlights the importance of ants."

The student smiles and states, "We also picked out where [the author] leaves readers with a final thought about ants."

"Wonderful," I reply. "Let's hear it."

The student reads the following passage from page 32 of the text:

The tunnel of time continues for the ants. Their hard work inspires people today, as it has for centuries. Look down on a warm day and you will probably find an ant. Drop a piece of food . . . and an ant will probably find you.

"Very nice," I respond. "What final thoughts does this passage leave readers with?"

Another student in the group answers: "It says that ants work hard and that their hard work inspires people. It also says that ants are easy to find."

"Good job," I tell the student. "The author of this book leaves readers with a final thought about the work ethic ants have. He also leaves us with a final thought about how ants can seem like they're everywhere. This author wants to us to think about ants' work ethics after we finish reading. He also wants us to always keep an eye out for ants, since they do sometimes seem like they're everywhere. Did you all like this conclusion?"

"Yeah," answers one student in the group. "It was a good way to show how important ants are."

I continue to circulate around the classroom, meeting with more groups and talking with them about the conclusions of the informational texts they've selected. After I've met with each group, I ask the groups to share their analysis by placing the charts they've completed on the document camera and telling the rest of the class how their book's conclusion highlights the significance of the book's topic and leaves readers with a final message or thought. Once all of the groups have shared their analyses, I praise the class: "All of our groups did such wonderful work today. You all did so well at the task of analyzing these published conclusions!"

Recommendations for Teaching Students about Crafting a Concluding Section

In this section, I describe a step-by-step instructional process to use when teaching students about crafting a concluding section. The instructional steps I recommend are: 1) Show students examples of effective conclusions from published informational texts and explain why they are effective; 2) Talk with students about why effective conclusions are important to strong informational writing; 3) Ask students to analyze how published conclusions meet the criteria for effective conclusions; 4) Have students create their own conclusions and analyze the effectiveness of those conclusions; and 5) Ask students to reflect on why well-crafted conclusions are important to effective informational writing. Each of these recommendations is described in detail in this section.

1. Show students examples of effective conclusions from published informational texts and explain why they are effective.

The first step in this instructional process is to show students examples of effective published conclusions and explain what makes those conclusions especially effective. Doing this provides students with "mentor" examples of strong conclusions, allowing them to observe and learn from the ways published authors craft the conclusions in their informational works. When I present strong published conclusions to my students, I place an example on a document camera and read it with them. After this, I explain that effective conclusions typically highlight the significance of the piece's topic and leave readers with a final thought or message about the topic; I then identify specific ways the conclusion I've shared with the students embodies these criteria.

For example, when recently working with a group of fifth graders on this topic, I showed them the conclusion from Jeanette Larson and Adrienne Yorinks' (2011) informational text *Hummingbirds* discussed earlier in this chapter and pointed out specific ways that the authors highlight the historical significance of hummingbirds, while also leaving readers with a final message about preserving the environment so that future generations can also enjoy hummingbirds. Showing students effective examples like this one and highlighting what the author does well provides them with a concrete model of what a strong conclusion looks like, as well as an explicit understanding of exactly what makes that example effective. When doing this with your students, remember to identify specific ways the author of the published conclusion you share with them highlights the importance of the topic and leaves readers with a final message; this will ensure the students' understanding of how published authors achieve these results in their works.

2. Talk with students about why effective conclusions are important to strong informational writing.

The next step of this instructional process builds off of the previous one, as it helps students understand why the attributes of an effective conclusion can improve the reader's experience. When I talk with students about the importance of effective conclusions to strong informational works, I explain why conclusions should highlight the significance of the piece's topic and leave readers with a final thought or message about the topic. This gets the students thinking metacognitively about the aspects of an effective conclusion. When I talk with students about a particular writing tool or strategy, I don't want them to simply do something in their writing because I've told them to; I want them to do it because they understand that writing in that way will make their work as strong as possible.

In a recent conversation with a group of fifth graders on this topic, I showed them a number of published conclusions and talked with them about why it's important that the authors of these conclusions have crafted them so effectively. One such conclusion came from Marilyn Singer's (2007) book *Venom*, an informational text about venomous animals. In the concluding section of this book, Singer writes:

> Unfortunately, many of these [venomous] animals are in danger. They are losing their habitats or are being sickened by pollutants and waste. They are being sold as pets—or killed by pets. They are slaughtered by people for their skins, for souvenirs, or simply for no better reason than because folks just don't like them.
>
> Unless we learn to appreciate these creatures, we won't safeguard them and their environments. If we don't safeguard them, we will never uncover or understand all of the marvels of venom and other biotoxins. We will lose the grace of a jellyfish, the trill of a toad, the beauty of a butterfly, the surprise of a snake, and even the awesome scariness of a big, hairy spider with its venomous fangs—and that would be a big loss indeed. (p. 89)

After showing the students this text, I explained that Singer emphasizes how venomous animals are special creatures with natural beauty and uniqueness, and that she leaves us with the message that we should appreciate and protect them in any way we can. I told the students that these ideas are important to the effectiveness of the conclusion because they show the importance of these animals and help the reader understand she or he can do something to help them. "Because this conclusion is so strong," I told the students, "it makes the whole book stronger. This is the last thing readers will read in this book, so it's important that the conclusion does a good job. A boring or uninformative conclusion wouldn't strengthen the book—it would weaken it." I also brought up William Zinsser's point that a conclusion should not simply summarize previously stated information. "If this conclusion just summarized," I explained, "it wouldn't highlight these important details and explain to us that it's important we help. A summary conclusion wouldn't be nearly as interesting to read, or as useful to the effectiveness of the book, as Singer's is."

3. Ask students to analyze how published conclusions meet the criteria for effective conclusions.

The third step of this instructional process calls for students to take more ownership of their learning by working individually or in small groups to find a conclusion from a published informational text and critique that conclusion by analyzing how it meets both criteria for effective conclusions. As described in this chapter's classroom snapshot, I recommend first showing students an example of what a completed version of this activity would look like, and then giving them the chart depicted in Figure 7.2 to fill out when completing the activity. While the students fill out the charts, I recommend meeting with them and asking them to justify their decisions with questions such as "Why do you think this excerpt highlights the importance of the topic?" and "How does this section reveal the final thoughts with which the author wants to leave us?" Questions such as these require students to support their answers and reveal the thinking behind the excerpts they recorded on their charts, helping to ensure that students think carefully about their choices and responses.

4. Have students create their own conclusions and analyze the effectiveness of those conclusions.

Next, I recommend asking students to create their own conclusions and analyze the effectiveness of those conclusions by identifying how they highlight the significance of their topics and leave readers with a final thought or message. This step of the instructional process requires students to apply this writing tool to their own works and to look at their own pieces critically, using the same analytical lens they previously applied to published examples. To help your students complete this step, I recommend first asking them to craft conclusions to informational pieces on which they're working, and to keep in mind the criteria for effective conclusions discussed in this chapter while doing so. As students write, confer with them, asking, "How does your conclusion highlight the significance of your topic?" and "What final message does your conclusion leave your reader with?" As students respond to these questions, ask them if they are happy with the information conveyed by their conclusions. For example, I'll ask my students, "Is the message that your conclusion gets across what you want your readers to take away from your piece?" If students don't believe the message in the conclusion is the one they want readers to consider, you can help them revise their work so that the desired and the actual text correspond.

For example, I recently conferred with a fifth grader who was writing an informational text on major historical figures in baseball. His piece described individuals such as Babe Ruth, Jackie Robinson, Mickey Mantle, and Derek Jeter, and talked about how all of them have made baseball important to America. When he examined his conclusion, he realized that it didn't convey the message he wanted it to. "I wanted my conclusion to leave readers thinking about how baseball will always be important to America and will always have new superstars," he told me. "But my conclusion right now doesn't really say that. It tells about the players I already talked about. I want to change that to telling readers that baseball will keep being important." This student made the decision to revise his conclusion by moving away from summarizing previously stated information and moving toward leaving readers with an important final message about baseball's future.

5. Ask students to reflect on why well-crafted conclusions are important to effective informational writing.

Finally, I recommend wrapping up this instructional process by asking students to reflect on why well-crafted conclusions are important to effective informational writing. Reflecting on the importance of strong conclusions helps students consider why this tool is especially useful to informational texts. When encouraging my students to reflect on the importance of strong conclusions, I ask them to draw on their experiences examining the conclusions of published texts as well as their own works. When recently working with a fifth-grade class on this topic, I asked them to respond to the following prompt:

You now know from our discussions and activities in our past several class meetings about the features of strong conclusions. You've looked for those features in published works as well as in your own writing. Now, I'd like you to think about this: why are strong conclusions so important to good informational writing?

I first asked the students to share their thoughts with their small group members; after a few minutes had passed, I asked for volunteers to share their insights with the whole class. I was pleased by the many insightful responses the students offered about the importance of well-crafted conclusions. One student explained that it's important that a conclusion "doesn't bore readers by summarizing, because just summarizing what you already wrote can be boring"; this student's response echoes Zinsser's call for conclusions to go beyond summarizing previously stated information. Another student explained that strong conclusions are useful because they highlight what's most essential to a piece of informational writing: "A good conclusion makes sure readers are paying attention to what's most important, not just random facts. A conclusion that just lists random facts wouldn't help the piece. It would just confuse readers." These students' responses reveal their understanding of the attributes of strong conclusions, as well as their understanding of why conclusions that embody these attributes are important to effective informational writing.

Final Thoughts on Crafting a Concluding Section

- ◆ The Common Core Writing Standards call for students to craft effective conclusions in their works, as Standards W.3.2d., W.4.2e, and W.5.2e discuss the importance of this concept.
- ◆ A concluding section of an informational text is a closing statement of one or more paragraphs that provides a sense of closure to the piece.
- ◆ An effective conclusion should do two things:
  - ◆ Highlight the significance of the piece's topic.
  - ◆ Leave readers with a final thought or message about this topic.
- ◆ Highlighting the significance of a topic is an important aspect of an effective conclusion because it emphasizes the value of the work to the reader.
- ◆ Leaving readers with a final thought or message related to the piece's topic is important to an effective conclusion because doing so gives readers something to continue to think about once they've finished reading the work.
- ◆ When teaching students about crafting a concluding section:
  - ◆ Show students examples of effective conclusions from published informational texts and explain why they are effective.
  - ◆ Talk with students about why effective conclusions are important to strong informational writing.
  - ◆ Ask students to analyze how published conclusions meet the criteria for effective conclusions.
  - ◆ Have students create their own conclusions and analyze the effectiveness of those conclusions.
  - ◆ Ask students to reflect on why well-crafted conclusions are important to effective informational writing.

8

Assessment Strategies

How Should We Assess Students' Informational Writings?

In this chapter, we'll explore some key concepts, strategies, and recommendations for you to use in your classrooms when assessing your students' informational writing. There are three key components of effective informational writing assessment that we'll discuss in this chapter: 1) Assessment of informational writing should be attribute focused, with specific evaluation criteria for each attribute; 2) Assessment of informational writing should be based on the instruction students have received; and 3) Assessment of informational writing should inform future instruction. Let's begin by exploring the first of these components, which emphasizes the attribute-focused nature of effective informational writing assessment.

Assessment of Informational Writing Should Be Attribute Focused, with Specific Evaluation Criteria for Each Attribute

Chapters One through Seven of this book each address specific components, or tools, of effective informational writing. I strongly recommend keeping the same tool-focused mindset when thinking about assessing students' informational works. When evaluating students' informational pieces, I suggest separately evaluating different tools used in their works. For example, when evaluating a student's informational writing, I'll give the student separate scores for distinct writing tools. For instance, a student's work might receive a score of four (out of four) for the quality of its introduction, but only a two for how well it develops the topic. This way, I can clearly communicate to students, parents, and administrators how well students have mastered each of the tools of informational writing.

I recently spoke with a group of elementary school teachers and administrators about this method of evaluating informational writing, and was especially pleased when one teacher told me, "I love this way of evaluating writing. I used to just give my students overall letter grades instead of breaking down their performance into different categories. Now, looking back, I can see how breaking down their performance into specific categories tells them what's working and what isn't." An administrator in the group added, "It's much better for me to know, 'This student needs help with writing conclusions' or 'This one needs support with linking ideas' than to just know, 'This student needs help with writing.' It's much better to break it down specifically." With these insights in mind, let's take a look at specific evaluation criteria you can use when assessing your students on each of the writing tools described in this book.

Introducing a Topic

The first standards-based tool described in this book is introducing a topic. Figure 8.1 contains a list of the evaluation criteria I use when assessing how well a student has introduced the topic in his or her informational piece. (Reproducible versions of all the figures depicted in this chapter are available in the Appendix.)

The evaluation questions for this writing tool relate to the key elements of effective introductions detailed earlier in this book. The scores I give my students on this aspect of their informational texts relate to how well their introductions engage the reader and introduce key content and information related to the piece's topic. Note that there is a space under these criteria for comments; I often use this space to make remarks about the effectiveness of the student's introduction and suggestions to keep in mind when creating future works.

Figure 8.1 Evaluation Criteria for Introducing a Topic

Writing Tool	Evaluation Criteria	Possible Points	Your Score
Introducing a topic	◆ Does the introduction engage the reader by grabbing his or her attention? ◆ Does the introduction introduce key content and information related to the topic of the piece?	4	
Comments:			

Grouping Related Information Together

The second tool for writing an effective informational text is the grouping together of related information. Since informational authors use organizational elements such as chapters, sections, and paragraphs to group related information together, the criteria I present here evaluate students on their uses of any of these organizational methods. (I explain to my elementary school students that they probably won't be using chapters in the pieces they write, but I want them to be aware of all of these possibilities for grouping related information together.) In addition, I evaluate the students on whether or not the information in the organizational elements they use is closely related. I included this evaluation component after noticing that some students would think they grouped related information together in their works because they used paragraphs, even though the paragraphs they created actually combined unrelated pieces of information. The two evaluation questions found in Figure 8.2 represent the criteria I use for evaluating how well students group related information together.

Adding Features that Aid Comprehension

The third informational writing tool described in this book is adding features that aid comprehension. When evaluating students' on their use of this writing tool, I consider the following criteria: 1) Does the text include features that aid comprehension?; 2) Are the features related to the piece's topic?; and 3) Do these features enhance the reader's understanding of the topic? These criteria allow me to consider the features on an increasing level of sophistication. First, I determine whether or not a student has included comprehension-aiding features. (It's important to be sure these features are present before evaluating them!) Then, if these features are included in the text, I examine them to conclude if they are clearly and closely related to the piece's topic. Sometimes students will include features that aren't closely related to

Figure 8.2 Evaluation Criteria for Grouping Related Information Together

Writing Tool	Evaluation Criteria	Possible Points	Your Score
Grouping related information together	◆ Does the author use organizational elements such as chapters, sections, and paragraphs to group related information together? ◆ Is the information in these organizational elements clearly related?	4	
Comments:			

Figure 8.3 Evaluation Criteria for Adding Features that Aid Comprehension

Writing Tool	Evaluation Criteria	Possible Points	Your Score
Adding features that aid comprehension	◆ Does the text include features such as headings, photographs, illustrations, charts, and graphs? ◆ Are these features clearly related to the piece's topic? ◆ Do these features enhance the reader's understanding of the topic?	4	
Comments:			

their piece. For instance, I recently helped a student who was working on an informational piece about snakes in the Southeastern United States. Some of the graphs and images she incorporated depicted snakes that were not among those that lived in this region. We worked together to ensure that the comprehension-aiding features she included corresponded directly with her topic.

Finally, I'll critique the features in the piece to evaluate whether or not they enhance the reader's understanding of the topic. When I do this, I'll ask myself what, if anything, these features do to increase the reader's understanding. For example, in Chapter Three of this book, I describe a conversation I had with an elementary school student who was writing an informational piece on snow leopards and planned to use a number of comprehension-aiding features to help readers understand the information in her piece as clearly as possible. This student planned to use specific headings such as "How Big Are Snow Leopards?" and "What Do Snow Leopards Eat?" to indicate what information was addressed in different sections of the paper. In addition, this student planned to use a chart to illustrate how the snow leopard population is declining. Features like these can clearly enhance a reader's understanding of a topic. Figure 8.3 depicts the evaluation criteria I use for determining how well students add features that aid comprehension.

Developing a Topic

Another tool on which to evaluate students' informational writings is developing a topic. This is an especially important component of effective informational text, as a piece with a clearly developed topic will provide readers with important facts and details about its subject. When

Figure 8.4 Evaluation Criteria for Developing a Topic

Writing Tool	Evaluation Criteria	Possible Points	Your Score
Developing a topic	◆ Does the text include information such as facts, definitions, details, quotations, and examples? ◆ Are these pieces of information clearly related to the piece's topic? ◆ Does this information help the reader understand the topic?	4	
Comments:			

evaluating students on this writing tool, I'll consider the following questions: 1) Does the text include information that develops the topic, such as facts, definitions, details, quotations, and examples?; 2) Are these pieces of information clearly related to the piece's topic?; and 3) Does this information help the reader understand the topic? These questions help me evaluate if the student has used information to develop a particular topic, if this information is relevant, and if the information is useful to the reader. I recently worked with an elementary school student who was writing an informational piece on Virginia Beach. She scored highly on this evaluation component because of the way she used details and examples to help readers understand the animal life, events, and activities associated with this beach. When I asked her about the way she developed her topic in this piece, the student explained, "I knew readers would know a lot about Virginia Beach if I used a lot of detail. If I didn't use details, they probably wouldn't." Figure 8.4 depicts the evaluation criteria I use when evaluating how well a student has developed a topic.

Linking Ideas

The writing concept of linking ideas is another important, standards-based tool to consider when evaluating students' informational writings. According to the CCSS, informational authors need to be able to link ideas "within and across categories of information" (Common Core State Standards, 2010). To do this, they need to be able to use words and phrases that indicate the relationships between the ideas conveyed in their works. When evaluating students on this concept, I ask myself: 1) Does the student's work include words and phrases that link the ideas in the piece; and 2) Do these words and phrases clearly show the relationship between

Figure 8.5 Evaluation Criteria for Linking Ideas

Writing Tool	Evaluation Criteria	Possible Points	Your Score
Linking ideas	◆ Does the text include words and phrases that link the ideas in the piece? ◆ Do these words and phrases clearly show the relationship between the linked ideas?	4	
Comments:			

the linked ideas? The second of these questions is especially important, as I want to be sure that the students are using idea-linking terms that accurately align with the information in their works. For example, if a student is attempting to link two unrelated ideas, I want to be sure that he is using language such as "however" or "on the other hand" that means that two ideas are distinct from one another. If the student is using terms like "in addition" or "also" to link contradictory or distinct ideas, the reader would be confused and have difficulty making sense of the piece. Figure 8.5 depicts the criteria I use when evaluating my students' use of this writing tool.

Using Precise Language and Domain-Specific Vocabulary
The next writing tool to consider when evaluating students' informational writing is the use of precise language and domain-specific vocabulary. This is a significant aspect of effective informational writing, as informational authors frequently address specialized topics, and therefore need to use specific terms related to those topics. When an informational author uses precise language and domain-specific vocabulary, his or her work will be as clear and specific as possible, and will express its ideas concisely. Recall the student work depicted in Chapter Six, in which a student explained that a volcano "erupted," and then, in another version of the sentence, wrote that the volcano "blew up." "Erupted" not only uses domain-specific vocabulary to describe the actions of the volcano, but it also conveys its message without using excess language. When evaluating informational writing on the use of precise language and domain-specific vocabulary, I ask myself the following questions: 1) Does the piece include precise language and domain-specific vocabulary when presenting information to the reader?; and 2) Is it clear that the precise language and domain-specific vocabulary used relates to the

Figure 8.6 Evaluation Criteria for Using Precise Language and Domain-Specific Vocabulary

Writing Tool	Evaluation Criteria	Possible Points	Your Score
Using precise language and domain-specific vocabulary	◆ Does the piece include precise language and domain-specific vocabulary when presenting information to the reader? ◆ Is it clear that the precise language and domain-specific vocabulary used relates to the author's message?	4	
Comments:			

author's message? These questions allow me to evaluate the students' works for the presence of these terms and the effectiveness with which they are used. I want to be sure that students are incorporating precise language and domain-specific vocabulary in ways that are accurate and that clearly get the piece's intended message across to the reader. The chart depicted in Figure 8.6 contains the criteria I use to evaluate students on this writing tool.

Crafting a Concluding Section

The final informational writing tool on which I evaluate my students' works is the quality of the concluding section. When assessing the quality of students' conclusions, I ask three questions about it: 1) Does the conclusion highlight the significance of the piece's topic?; 2) Does the conclusion leave readers with a final thought or message about the topic?; and 3) Does the conclusion go beyond summarizing the paper's content? Conclusions that score highly on these evaluation criteria will keep readers engaged through the end of the piece, while also ensuring that even the final section of the paper provides important information. I recently worked with a student who was crafting a concluding section to an informational piece on hybrid cars. When I asked her about her goals for the paper's conclusion, she explained, "I want to make it really clear that hybrid cars are great ways to help the environment. I don't want to just summarize things I've already said, like how they work and the different kinds of hybrids there are." This student's comments reveal her desire to go beyond summarizing her piece's content in her conclusion, and also indicate how she will highlight the significance of hybrid cars and leave readers with a final message about them. Figure 8.7 illustrates the evaluation criteria I use when critiquing a piece's conclusion.

Figure 8.7 Evaluation Criteria for Crafting a Concluding Section

Writing Tool	Evaluation Criteria	Possible Points	Your Score
Crafting a concluding section	◆ Does the conclusion highlight the significance of the piece's topic? ◆ Does the conclusion leave readers with a final thought or message about the topic? ◆ Does the conclusion go beyond summarizing the paper's content?	4	
Comments:			

A Note on Using These Evaluation Criteria

While this evaluation approach is designed to assess students on distinct writing tools, note that you don't have to always evaluate students on all seven tools at once. I like to begin a unit on informational writing by assessing students' works on two fairly basic writing tools, such as introducing a topic and grouping related information together. Once it seems like students have mastered these concepts, I introduce new, slightly more complex tools, such as adding features that aid comprehension and using precise language and domain-specific vocabulary, and evaluate the students' works on their uses of these concepts as well. Evaluating students on specific writing tools also presents opportunities for differentiation: while some students might complete an informational writing project and be ready to be evaluated on all seven of the tools described in this chapter, others might be best served by being evaluated on four or five at that particular time and being evaluated on the others later in the school year when they've had more time to develop as writers. Next, let's consider another important component of assessing students' informational writings: the link between assessment and instruction.

Assessment of Informational Writing Should Be Based on the Instruction Students Have Received

I strongly believe that assessment of student writing should be based on the instruction students have received. Suzanne Bratcher and Linda Ryan, in their book, *Evaluating Children's Writing* (2004), urge all educators to "never grade on something you've never taught" (p. 129) explaining that doing so places students in an unfair position when it comes to assessment and evaluation. They explain that, to maximize our students' chances of success, we should ensure that we are evaluating them on specific writing concepts and strategies that we have helped them understand. Bratcher and Ryan's advice aligns with the toolkit-oriented instructional approach outlined in this book: once we've presented specific informational writing strategies to students as tools for effective writing; shown students examples of mentor texts that utilize these concepts; discussed their importance; and asked students to analyze, use, and reflect on these strategies, then it is fair for us to evaluate students on these writing concepts.

The idea of basing assessment on instruction students have received came up during one of my recent conversations with teachers about effective informational writing instruction. As one teacher in the group aptly put it, "If we teach students writing strategies and then assess them [on those strategies], we're helping them be successful. We're showing them what they need to know and then seeing if they know it." This teacher's comment is especially significant because of its focus on facilitating students' successes. Through the instructional practices described in this book, we can help our students learn how to apply specific writing tools to their informational works. Once we've discussed these tools with our students, we can evaluate how well they've used them. In the next section of this chapter, we'll discuss the idea of using our assessments of students' informational writing to inform our future instruction.

Assessment of Informational Writing Should Inform Future Instruction

I highly recommend using your assessments of your students' informational writings to inform your future instruction. This suggestion works in tandem with the previous idea that the assessment of our students should be based on our instruction. I see these two assessment strategies as being on the same continuum: once we assess our students on writing tools that we have taught them, we can then use their performances on these assessments to determine what tools to target in our future lessons and activities. For example, I recently spoke with a fourth-grade teacher who explained how she was going to use the results of a recent assessment to guide her future instruction: "My students did really nicely at most of the writing strategies I taught them, but they did struggle with two: linking ideas and using specific vocabulary. I'm going to spend a lot more time in the coming weeks on getting them to link ideas and use specific vocabulary."

The NCTE/IRA Standards for the Assessment of Reading and Writing (2009) describe the importance of using assessment to inform instruction, asserting that "the primary purpose of assessment is to improve teaching and learning." The standards explain that an effective assessment practice "must inform instruction and lead to improved teaching and learning" (NCTE/IRA, 2009). The insights the fourth-grade teacher in the preceding paragraph shared exemplify this practice; this teacher analyzed her students' performances on an informational writing assessment and used those performances to determine what instructional areas required further attention. Her interest in using assessment results to guide her instruction will ultimately enhance her students' learning experiences.

Final Thoughts on Assessing Students' Informational Writings

- ◆ Assessment of informational writing should be attribute focused, with specific evaluation criteria for each attribute:
  - ◆ Each of the writing tools discussed in this book represents a separate writing attribute on which to evaluate students.
  - ◆ Evaluating students on specific attributes provides clear feedback on which writing tools they have mastered and which require further attention.
  - ◆ Remember that you don't need to evaluate students on all seven writing tools described in this book at one time. I like to begin by assessing students' works on two fairly basic writing tools, then adding more complex ones as time goes on.
- ◆ Assessment of informational writing should be based on the instruction students have received.
- ◆ Assessment of informational writing should inform future instruction.

9

Final Thoughts and Tips for Classroom Practice

How Can We Put the Ideas in This Book into Practice?

Let's reflect back on the vignette that begins the introductory chapter of this book, which describes elementary school teachers' concerns about teaching informational writing. In response to these teachers' anxieties, I explained to them that students can become strong *writers* of informational texts once they become strong *readers* of informational texts. Once students understand what strong informational writing looks like and are aware of the writing tools and strategies effective informational authors use in their works, the students can apply those same strategies to the informational pieces that they create. Since the Common Core Standards emphasize informational reading and writing—literacy components that, according to research (Duke, 2000) frequently have not received adequate attention—it is especially important to help students understand and use the tools needed to craft strong informational texts.

In this chapter, we'll examine some especially important tips for putting the ideas in this book into practice. These recommendations, which focus on the importance of helping students understand and use the tools of effective informational writing, are:

- Show students published examples of specific informational writing tools.
- Talk with students about why each one of these writing tools is important to effective informational writing.
- Engage students in an activity in which they analyze the importance of an informational writing tool.

- Ask students to apply specific informational writing tools to their own works.
- Have students reflect on the importance of specific tools to effective informational writing.
- Evaluate students on their uses of specific informational writing tools.

Let's take a look at each of these recommendations in more detail.

Recommendation One: Show Students Published Examples of Specific Informational Writing Tools

The first step to helping students understand and use specific informational writing strategies is to show them published examples—also known as mentor texts—of each of these writing tools. Like the process of building a house, effective writing instruction must begin by laying a strong foundation, and showing students published examples of specific writing strategies is an excellent way to establish that foundation. Each chapter in this book contains specific published examples that you can draw from when showing your students mentor texts related to a specific concept. However, remember to also keep your students' interests in mind when presenting them with these mentor texts. If you have a number of students interested in wolves, for example, then examine some published informational texts about wolves and find examples of specific informational writing strategies to point out to your students. When you show your students these published examples, be sure to clearly identify the specific writing strategy you want them to focus on. For example, if you want your students to hone in on the language in a particular passage that links ideas, then make sure that they know which words and phrases the author uses to link these ideas. This provides a good transition to the next key recommendation we'll discuss: talking with students about the importance of specific writing tools.

Recommendation Two: Talk with Students about Why Each One of These Writing Tools Is Important to Effective Informational Writing

Once you've shown students published examples of specific writing strategies, the next step is to talk with them about why each particular strategy is important to effective informational writing. The specific points you make will vary with each writing strategy, but the overall message you'll want to convey to your students is that all of the writing strategies you're showing them are important tools that effective informational authors use to make their works as strong as possible. One way to illustrate this is to show students how informational works would look with specific writing tools and then draw comparisons to how they look without those tools. For example, when talking with your students about the importance of using precise language and domain-specific vocabulary, I recommend showing your students a sentence from a published work that contains domain-specific vocabulary and comparing it with a revised version of that sentence that uses vague and general language instead of these specific terms. As you compare these examples, think aloud about the differences between them and how the domain-specific vocabulary enhances your experience reading the original text. While thinking aloud, you can emphasize the importance of the particular writing concept you are describing. For example, if you are talking about precise language and domain-specific vocabulary, you can use the think-aloud to assert that these types of language and vocabulary are important to effective informational writing because they make a piece as clear and specific as possible and allow writers to express their ideas concisely. No matter which writing tool you are describing, comparing examples with and without the tool and thinking aloud about how the two examples are different can help students grasp the importance of the concept.

Recommendation Three: Engage Students in an Activity in Which They Analyze the Importance of an Informational Writing Tool

The next step in this series of instructional steps is to involve the students in an activity in which they analyze the significance of a specific informational writing tool. This step is related to the gradual release of responsibility, described in this book's Introduction, in which students gradually take increased ownership of and responsibility for their learning. Since at this point in the process, you will have shown the students examples of specific writing tools and discussed with them the importance of those tools to effective informational writing, they will now be ready to take on more responsibility. To facilitate this increased responsibility, I like to give students a task designed to help them further understand why a particular informational writing tool is so significant.

The specific activity you'll give your students will vary based on the writing concept being addressed. Some activities are best conducted as small group work, while others are most effectively done as whole-class discussions. For example, when working with my fifth-grade students on the writing concept of conclusions, I asked them to work in small groups to analyze how published authors' conclusions meet the criteria for effective conclusions that we had discussed as a class. This activity was designed to help students think about how published authors craft effective conclusions and why those conclusions enhance the texts in which they are found. In another instance, when helping a class of third graders understand the importance of introducing a topic, I showed the whole class a published text with and without its introductory paragraph and asked them to consider how the piece differs without its introduction. Considering these examples helped the students think about why introductions are so important to strong informational writing. No matter which strategy you address or whether the activity the students do is completed in small groups, individually, or as a whole class, engaging them in an activity that increases the amount of responsibility placed on them helps them consider the importance of the writing tool you're discussing.

Recommendation Four: Ask Students to Apply Specific Informational Writing Tools to Their Own Works

This instructional recommendation places even more responsibility on the students by asking them to work individually to apply specific informational writing tools to their own works. I like to present this instructional step to my students as something they've "earned" by completing the previous stages. For example, if my students are studying the writing tool of linking ideas, I'll say: "Through your work in our past several classes, you've shown me that you really understand what it means to link ideas in a piece of informational writing. Now, you're ready to use this writing tool on your own in the pieces of writing you're creating." I'll then ask the students to work on the pieces of informational writing they are composing at the time and to pay special attention to using language that links idea while they are writing. While the students write, I hold one-on-one writing conferences in which I check in with each of them and see how they are implementing the focal concept in their writing. These conferences provide excellent opportunities for individualized instruction that focuses on students' specific strengths and weaknesses.

Recommendation Five: Have Students Reflect on the Importance of Specific Tools to Effective Informational Writing

Now that the students have worked on applying specific writing tools to the informational text that they're composing, I suggest asking each of them to reflect on the importance of a particular writing tool to effective informational texts. For example, if students have just finished focusing on adding features that aid comprehension of their works, I recommend presenting them with a reflection question (or a group of questions) that asks them to consider the importance of this concept to strong informational writing. When working on this concept with my students, I'll pose the following reflection questions: 1) What features that aid comprehension did you add to your informational writing? and 2) How can each of these features help readers understand the information in your piece?

These questions require students to not only identify the specific comprehension-aiding tools they included in their works, but to also discuss how each of these tools can enhance the reader's understanding. When responding to questions such as these, students are forced to consider the usefulness of a particular writing tool to a piece of informational writing, which enhances students' metacognitive awareness of why each of these concepts is important to effective informational writing. Students with strong awareness of the usefulness and importance of particular writing concepts can understand why each of these concepts is a specific tool that writers useful purposefully and with clear understandings of their benefits.

Recommendation Six: Evaluate Students on Their Uses of Specific Informational Writing Tools

The final step of this instructional process concerns the assessment of students' informational works: when evaluating students' informational writings, I recommend evaluating them on their uses of specific informational writing tools. I suggest using the specific criteria described in Chapter Eight to gauge students' mastery of the particular writing strategies discussed in this book. As discussed in Chapter Eight, evaluating students on particular tools helps them know how well they've mastered specific writing concepts, and also clearly communicates to other interested individuals—such as parents, administrators, and other teachers—exactly what a student's areas of strength and need are.

Evaluating students on particular tools helps them see writing as a set of skills, a mindset that can facilitate their improvement. I recently spoke with a fourth grader who told me, "I used to think I just wasn't a good writer, but now I know that I'm good at some parts of writing and not at others. I know what parts of writing I can get better at." This student's statement is especially significant because it illustrates his understanding that being a good writer involves mastering specific skills or tools. Armed with this knowledge, he understands which writing tools represent his strengths and which represent areas of future growth. Remember that you don't need to evaluate all of the writing tools described in this book at the same time. Instead, you can begin by evaluating students on a select number of tools (I often start with two) and then introduce new, slightly more complex ones as time goes and evaluate them accordingly. This will provide specific evaluation feedback without overwhelming the students.

Final Thoughts on the Informational Writing Toolkit

The tools of informational writing described in this book represent ways to help your students become effective informational authors. As you work with your students on these concepts, emphasize to them that each concept is a tool of effective informational writing that authors use purposefully and with a clear understanding of its uses and benefits. Show your students examples from mentor texts of these writing tools, explain the importance of each of them, and gradually release responsibility onto the students as they analyze the importance of each concept, use it on their own, and reflect on its importance. Remember that you aren't teaching these informational writing tools to your students alone: instead, you have numerous mentor texts at your fingertips that you can use to help your students grasp these writing concepts and add them to their informational writing toolkits.

Section **3**

Resources

References

Arnold, C. (1980). *Electric fish.* New York, NY: William Morrow and Company.

Arnold, C. (1997). *African animals.* New York, NY: Morrow Junior Books.

Binns, T. B. (2005). *The Vikings.* Minneapolis, MN: Compass Point Books.

Bratcher, S., & Ryan, L. (2004). *Evaluating children's writing: A handbook of grading choices for classroom teachers* (2nd ed.). Mahwah, NJ: Lawrence Erlbaum.

Brown, M. B. (1992). *Wings along the waterway.* New York, NY: Orchard Books.

Caswell, L. J., & Duke, N. K. (1998). Non-narrative as a catalyst for literacy development. *Language Arts, 75* (2), 108–117.

Common Core State Standards Initiative. (2010). Common core state standards for English language arts. Retrieved from: www.corestandards. org/ELA-Literacy.

Culham, R. (2003). *6 + 1 traits of writing.* New York, NY: Scholastic.

Davis, G. W. (1997). *Coral reef.* New York, NY: Children's Press.

Dinn, S. (1996). *Hearts of gold.* Woodbridge, CT: Blackbirch Press.

Duke, N. K. (2000). 3.6 minutes per day: The scarcity of informational texts in first grade. *Reading Research Quarterly, 35* (2), 202–224.

Fisher, D., & Frey, N. (2003). Writing instruction for struggling adolescent readers: A gradual release model. *Journal of Adolescent and Adult Literacy, 46* (5), 396–407.

Flavell, J. H. (1979). Metacognition and cognitive monitoring. *American Psychologist, 34,* 906–911.

Fletcher, R., & Portalupi, J. (2001). *Writing workshop: The essential guide.* Portsmouth, NH: Heinemann.

Fradin, J., & Fradin, D. (2007). *Volcanoes: Witness to disaster.* Washington, DC: National Geographic Society.

Giblin, J. C. (1997). *Charles A. Lindbergh: A human hero.* New York, NY: Clarion Books.

Gilpin, D. (2006). *Snails, shellfish, & other mollusks.* Minneapolis, MN: Compass Point Books.

Gilpin, D. (2006). *Starfish, urchins, & other echinoderms.* Minneapolis, MN: Compass Point Books.

Guthrie, J. T., & Alao, S. (1987). Designing contexts to increase motivations for reading. *Educational Psychologist, 32* (2), 95–105.

Hoare, S. (1998). *The world of caves, mines, and tunnels.* New York, NY: Peter Bedrick Books.

Krensky, S. (2007). *The mummy.* Minneapolis, MN: Lerner Publications Company.

Ladson-Billins, G. (1995). But that's just good teaching! The case for culturally relevant pedagogy. *Theory into Practice, 34* (3), 159–165.

La Pierre, Y. (2008). *Neandertals: A prehistoric puzzle.* Minneapolis, MN: Twenty-First Century Books.

Larson, J., & Yorinks, A. (2011). *Hummingbirds.* Watertown, MA: Charlesbridge.

Lucas, E. (1991). *Acid rain.* Chicago, IL: Children's Press.

Macquitty, M. (2004). *Shark.* New York, NY: DK Publishing.

Markle, S. (2004). *Outside and inside killer bees.* New York, NY: Walker and Company.

Masoff, J. (2006). *Oh, yikes: History's grossest, wackiest moments.* New York, NY: Workman.

McGovern, A. (1992). *If you lived in Colonial Times.* New York, NY: Scholastic.

McMillan, B., & Musick, J. A. (2007). *Oceans.* New York, NY: Simon & Schuster Books for Young Readers.

Micucci, C. (2003). *The life and times of the ant.* Boston, MA: Houghton Mifflin Company.

Millard, A. (1996). *Pyramids.* New York, NY: Kingfisher.

Patent, D. H. (1981). *Horses of America.* New York, NY: Holiday House.

National Council of Teachers of English/International Reading Association (2009). *NCTE/IRA standards for the assessment of reading and writing.* Retrieved from: www.ncte.org/standards/assessmentstandards.

Newkirk, T. (1989). *More than stories: The range of children's writing.* Portsmouth, NH: Heinemann.

Ramen, F. (2005). *North America before Columbus.* New York, NY: Rosen.

Ray, K. W. (1999). *Wondrous words: Writers and writing in the elementary classroom.* Urbana, IL: National Council of Teachers of English.

Riley, P. (1998). *Food chains.* Danbury, CT: Franklin Watts.

Sattler, H. R. (1989). *The book of eagles.* New York, NY: Lothrop, Lee & Shepard Books.

Singer, M. (2007). *Venom.* Plain City, OH: Darby Creek Publishing.

Silverstein, A., Silverstein, V., & Nunn, L. S. (1998). *Symbiosis.* Brookfield, CT: Twenty-First Century Books.

Silverstein, A., Silverstein, V., & Nunn, L. S. (1998). *The grizzly bear.* Brookfield, CT: The Millbrook Press.

Spilsbury, L., & Spilsbury, R. (2003). *Crushing avalanches.* Chicago, IL: Heinemann Library.

Snodgrass, M. E. (1991). *Air pollution.* Marco, FL: Bancroft-Sage.

Stewart, M. (2001). *Reptiles.* New York, NY: Children's Press.

Stille, D. R. (2004). *Cheetahs.* Minneapolis, MN: Compass Point Books.

Todd, A. M. (2003). *Sitting Bull.* Mankato, MN: Blue Earth Books.

Wahl, G. (2014). World Cup preview 2014. *Sports Illustrated, 120* (23), 38–44.

Wilhelm, J. (2001). *Improving comprehension with think-aloud strategies.* New York, NY: Scholastic.

Woods, M., & Woods, M. B. (2007). *Tsunamis.* Minneapolis, MN: Lerner Publications Company.

Zimmerman, K. (2004). *Steam locomotives.* Honesdale, PA: Boyds Mills Press.

Zinsser. W. (2006). *On writing well: 30th anniversary edition.* New York, NY: Harper Perennial.

Annotated Bibliography

This annotated bibliography contains the following information: 1) The titles and authors of the informational works that I describe in this book as exemplars of the tools of effective informational writing; 2) A tool of effective informational writing found in each work; 3) The Common Core Writing Standards associated with that tool; 4) An excerpt from that work, found earlier in this book, that demonstrates exactly how the author uses that informational writing tool; and 5) Information on which chapter in this book the concept is discussed (in case you want to refer back to the text for more information on a concept).

The annotated bibliography is designed to make this book as user friendly as possible. It is organized alphabetically by author's last name, and each entry includes important details designed to help you use these published works to teach your students about the tools of informational writing.

Arnold, C. (1980). *Electric fish.* New York, NY: William Morrow and Company.
Title: Electric Fish
Author: Caroline Arnold
Informational Writing Tool: Introducing a topic
Related Common Core Standards: W.3.2a, W.4.2a, W.5.2a
Excerpt that Demonstrates Concept:

"Did you know that an electric eel can produce enough electricity to shock a horse? Did you know that a shark is able to find a fish hidden in the sand because it can feel a small amount of electricity given off by the fish? Did you know that some fish can 'talk' to each other with electric signals? All of these fish have a unique sensitivity to electricity.
    Some fish can produce an electric current. The electricity is made by a special part of the fish's body called an 'electric organ.' The electric organ can be very big or very small." (pp. 3–4)

Discussed in Chapter: One

Arnold, C. (1997). *African animals.* New York, NY: Morrow Junior Books.

Title: *African Animals*
Author: Caroline Arnold
Informational Writing Tool: Grouping related information together
Related Common Core Standards: W.3.2a, W.4.2a, W.5.2a
Excerpt that Demonstrates Concept:

"Elephants are the heaviest of all land animals. Some adults weight more than fourteen thousand pounds. That's as much as a medium-sized truck! Because elephants are so big, other animals cannot easily harm them." (p. 14)

Discussed in Chapter: Two

Binns, T.B. (2005). *The Vikings.* Minneapolis, MN: Compass Point Books.
Title: *The Vikings*
Author: Tristan B. Binns
Informational Writing Tool: Developing a topic
Related Common Core Standards: W.3.2b, W.4.2b, W.5.2b
Excerpt that Demonstrates Concept:

"Vikings used their ships to take trade goods along the rivers that ran into Russia. They took wax, honey, slaves, and furs to trade for luxuries such as jewelry, wine, silk, and spices." (p. 20)

Discussed in Chapter: Four

Brown, M. B. (1992). *Wings along the waterway.* New York, NY: Orchard Books.
Title: *Wings along the Waterway*
Author: Mary Barrett Brown
Informational Writing Tool: Crafting a concluding section
Related Common Core Standards: W.3.2d., W.4.2, W5.2e
Excerpt that Demonstrates Concept:

"Although water birds are resourceful, they need our attention to survive. Civilization may be their greatest threat. Encroachment upon the wetlands, and drainage of the birds' habitat can quickly reduce their population. Pollution and pesticides also threaten their survival. And so we observe them and learn, and in the process we discover the sense of wonder these birds and their special world can inspire. As long as the waterways last, there will be water birds." (p. 77)

Discussed in Chapter: Seven

Davis, G.W. (1997). *Coral reef*. New York, NY: Children's Press.
Title: *Coral Reef*
Author: Gary W. Davis
Informational Writing Tool: Introducing a topic
Related Common Core Standards: W.3.2a, W.4.2a, W.5.2a
Excerpt that Demonstrates Concept:

"The waters of the Caribbean Sea are warm and clear. On the surface, everything appears peaceful. But just below, rising from the bottom of the sea, there is a very busy place. It is the underwater community of the coral reef." (p. 4)

Discussed in Chapter: One

Dinn, S. (1996). *Hearts of gold*. Woodbridge, CT: Blackbirch Press.
Title: *Hearts of Gold*
Author: Sheila Dinn
Informational Writing Tool: Developing a topic
Related Common Core Standards: W3.2b, W4.2b, W5.2b
Excerpt that Demonstrates Concept:

"Sports lets me be proud of who I am and what I can do . . . plus it shows me what I can do with hard work." (p. 51)

Discussed in Chapter: Four

Fradin, J., & Fradin, D. (2007). *Volcanoes: Witness to disaster*. Washington, DC: National Geographic Society.
Title: *Volcanoes: Witness to Disaster*
Authors: Judy and Dennis Fradin
Informational Writing Tool: Using precise language and domain-specific vocabulary
Related Common Core Standards: W.4.2d, W.5.2d
Excerpt that Demonstrates Concept:

"By April, as magma and gas built up intense pressure inside, the mountain had begun to bulge." (p. 27)

Discussed in Chapter: Six

Giblin, J. C. (1997). *Charles A. Lindbergh: A human hero.* New York, NY: Clarion Books.
Title: *Charles A. Lindbergh: A Human Hero*
Author: James Cross Giblin
Informational Writing Tool: Developing a topic
Related Common Core Standards: W.3.2b, W.4.2b, W5.2b
Excerpt that Demonstrates Concept:

"All the equipment for the flight had been assembled—Charles's flight suit, water canteens, Army rations, a rubber raft, a repair kit, and ref flairs in case the plane went down in the ocean and Charles had to signal from the raft." (p. 52)

Discussed in Chapter: Four

Gilpin, D. (2006). *Snails, shellfish, & other mollusks.* Minneapolis, MN: Compass Point Books.
Title: *Snails, Shellfish, & Other Mollusks*
Author: Daniel Gilpin
Informational Writing Tool: Linking ideas
Related Common Core Standards: W.3.2c, W.4.2c, W.5.2c
Excerpt that Demonstrates Concept:

"Slugs and snails are small, slow-moving, silent creatures. Also, they are most active at night, so they are often overlooked." (p. 26)

Discussed in Chapter: Five

Gilpin, D. (2006). *Starfish, urchins, & other echinoderms.* Minneapolis, MN: Compass Point Books.
Title: *Starfish, Urchins, & Other Echinoderms*
Author: Daniel Gilpin
Informational Writing Tool: Using precise language and domain-specific vocabulary
Related Common Core Standards: W.4.2d, W.5.2d
Excerpt that Demonstrates Concept:

"Starfish have incredible powers of regeneration. If they lose a limb to a predator, they soon grow another one." (p. 13)

Discussed in Chapter: Six

Hoare, S. (1998). *The world of caves, mines, and tunnels.* New York, NY: Peter Bedrick Books.
Title: *The World of Caves, Mines, and Tunnels*
Author: Stephen Hoare
Informational Writing Tool: Developing a topic
Related Common Core Standards: W.3.2b, W.4.2b, W.5.2b
Excerpt that Demonstrates Concept:

"Once lines of trenches had been dug, the next most important thing was to excavate living quarters and command posts. These were called 'dug-outs' and the miners who were commissioned to do the digging were known as 'sappers.' They tunneled 35 feet below the level of the trench and reinforced the roof with steel bars, concrete, and sand bags." (p. 28)

Discussed in Chapter: Four

Krensky, S. (2007). *The mummy.* Minneapolis, MN: Lerner Publications Company.
Title: *The Mummy*
Author: Stephen Krensky
Informational Writing Tool: Adding features that aid comprehension
Related Common Core Standards: W.3.2a, W.4.2a, W.5.2a
Excerpts that Demonstrate Concept:

"The Science of Mummification" (p. 19) (Section heading)
    "Ancient Egyptians took great care to properly prepare their dead for the afterlife. In the image below, a priest wraps a dead body in strips of clean linen." (p. 21) (Illustration caption)

Discussed in Chapter: Three

La Pierre, Y. (2008). *Neandertals: A prehistoric puzzle.* Minneapolis, MN: Twenty-First Century Books.
Title: *Neandertals: A Prehistoric Puzzle*
Author: Yvette La Pierre
Informational Writing Tool: Crafting a concluding section
Related Common Core Standards: W.3.2d, W.4.2e, W.5.2e
Excerpt that Demonstrates Concept:

"As our closest relatives and the last human species we shared the world with, we will always be fascinated with Neandertals.

And perhaps it's human nature to be most interested in comparing them to us, to use Neandertals to better understand ourselves. So researchers will continue to look for clues to who the Neandertals were, how they lived, and why they disappeared." (p. 101)

Discussed in Chapter: Seven

Larson, J., & Yorinks, A. (2011). *Hummingbirds.* Watertown, MA: Charlesbridge.
Title: *Hummingbirds*
Authors: Jeanette Larson and Adrienne Yorinks
Informational Writing Tool: Crafting a concluding section
Related Common Core Standards: W.3.2d, W.4.2e, W.5.2e
Excerpt that Demonstrates Concept:

"Hummingbirds have been objects of fascination for centuries . . . the existence of hummingbirds is documented in pre-Columbian artifacts and artwork . . . Though tenacious, hummingbirds are still small birds, dependent on the environment for their survival. We need to be vigilant so that hundreds of years from now, when other children are studying hummingbirds, they will still be able to see these remarkable creatures with their own eyes." (p. 54)

Discussed in Chapter: Seven

Lucas, E. (1991). *Acid rain.* Chicago, IL: Children's Press.
Title: *Acid Rain*
Author: Eileen Lucas
Informational Writing Tool: Developing a topic
Related Common Core Standards: W.3.2b, W.4.2b, W.5.2b
Excerpts that Demonstrate Concept:

"Acid rain is rain, snow, sleet, or other forms of precipitation that have a higher acid content than normal. Some acids occur naturally in the atmosphere, but many others are the result of human activities. When these acids collect in the atmosphere, they combine with moisture in the air and the result is rain that is sometimes as acid as vinegar." (p. 9)

"Coal, oil, and natural gas are called fossil fuels. They were formed over millions of years from the remains of once-living trees, other plants, and animals. These living things died and fell into the swamps that covered ancient Earth. Year by year, century by century, more living things fell on top of the older ones. Over millions of years, the organic (once living) material was compressed by the weight above it and was gradually changed into the fossil fuels that we now remove from the earth for use in producing energy." (p. 11)

Discussed in Chapter: Four

Macquitty, M. (2004). *Shark.* New York, NY: DK Publishing.
Title: *Shark*
Author: Miranda Macquitty
Informational Writing Tool: Using precise language and domain-specific vocabulary
Related Common Core Standards: W.4.2d, W.5.2d
Excerpt that Demonstrates Concept:

"To breathe, sharks have gills that absorb oxygen from the water and release carbon dioxide back into it." (p. 10)

Discussed in Chapter: Six

Markle, S. (2004). *Outside and inside killer bees.* New York, NY: Walker and Company.
Title: *Outside and Inside Killer Bees*
Author: Sandra Markle
Informational Writing Tool: Linking ideas
Related Common Core Standards: W.3.2c, W.4.2c, W.5.2c
Excerpt that Demonstrates Concept:

"An Africanized bee's antennas are even more sensitive than those of European honeybees. However, the antennas of both kinds of bees look the same." (p. 11)

Discussed in Chapter: Five

Masoff, J. (2006). *Oh, yikes: History's grossest, wackiest moments.* New York, NY: Workman.
Title: *Oh, Yikes: History's Grossest, Wackiest Moments*
Author: Joy Masoff
Informational Writing Tool: Crafting a concluding section

Related Common Core Standards: W.3.2d, W.4.2e, W.5.2e
Excerpt that Demonstrates Concept:

"Without Attila, the Hunnish empire soon crumbled. But new cities had been created because of him—and the continent of Europe—sliced up by a short, eye-rolling ruler with a rusty sword—would never be the same." (p. 4)

Discussed in Chapter: Introduction

McGovern, A. (1992). *If you lived in Colonial Times*. New York, NY: Scholastic.
Title: *If You Lived in Colonial Times*
Author: Ann McGovern
Informational Writing Tool: Linking ideas
Related Common Core Standards: W.3.2c, W.4.2c, W.5.2c
Excerpt that Demonstrates Concept:

"If the town crier had special news to tell, he rang a bell or banged on a drum. Then people ran to hear what he was saying. Another way to hear the news was to go the village inn." (p. 62)

Discussed in Chapter: Five

McMillan, B., & Musick, J. A. (2007). *Oceans*. New York, NY: Simon & Schuster Books for Young Readers.
Title: *Oceans*
Authors: Beverly McMillan and John Musick
Informational Writing Tool: Linking ideas
Related Common Core Standards: W.3.2c, W.4.2c, W.5.2c
Excerpt that Demonstrates Concept:

"Old ships . . . provide homes for many forms of ocean life. For example, sea anemones and some mollusks live only where they can attach to a hard surface, and some fish only where they can hide." (p. 24)

Discussed in Chapter: Five

Micucci, C. (2003). *The life and times of the ant.* Boston, MA: Houghton Mifflin Company.
Title: *The Life and Times of the Ant*
Author: Charles Micucci
Informational Writing Tool: Crafting a concluding section
Related Common Core Standards: W.3.2d, W.4.2e, W.5.2e
Excerpt that Demonstrates Concept:

"Ants evolved from wasps more than 100 million years ago. They have been dodging footsteps ever since. As dinosaurs thundered above ground, ants dug out a home below. The mighty dinosaurs are long gone, but the little ant has survived . . . The tunnel of time continues for the ants. Their hard work inspires people today, as it has for centuries. Look down on a warm day and you will probably find an ant. Drop a piece of food . . . and an ant will probably find you." (pp. 30–32)

Discussed in Chapter: Seven

Millard, A. (1996). *Pyramids.* New York, NY: Kingfisher.
Title: *Pyramids*
Author: Anne Millard
Informational Writing Tool: Grouping related information together
Related Common Core Standards: W.3.2a, W.4.2a, W.5.2a
Excerpt that Demonstrates Concept:

"The pyramids at Giza were built by Khufu, his son Khafre, and grandson Mekaure. Khufu's, the Great Pyramid, is the largest. It is 482 feet (147 m) tall and built with about 2,300,000 blocks." (p. 26)

Discussed in Chapter: Two

Patent, D. H. (1981). *Horses of America.* New York, NY: Holiday House.
Title: *Horses of America*
Author: Dorothy Hinshaw Patent
Informational Writing Tool: Crafting a concluding section
Related Common Core Standards: W.3.2d, W.4.2e, W.5.2e
Excerpt that Demonstrates Concept:

"Horses have always been important in our country. They helped people explore and settle the land. They still work on farms and ranches. And they help people enjoy life by providing exciting competition, pleasant riding, and loving friendship. Because of their strength, loyalty, and beauty, horses will continue to play important roles in human life." (p. 76)

Discussed in Chapter: Seven

Ramen, F. (2005). *North America before Columbus.* New York, NY: Rosen.
Title: *North America before Columbus*
Author: Fred Ramen
Informational Writing Tool: Grouping related information together
Related Common Core Standards: W.3.2a, W.4.2a, W.5.2a
Excerpts that Demonstrate Concept:

"Native Tribes of the Southwest" (p. 29) (Chapter title)
   "Great secrecy was attached to Pueblo rituals. Each village had its own interpretation of the rites to be followed. The men who performed the ceremonies were members of secret societies that only slowly revealed their rituals to the younger men of the tribe." (p. 31) (Paragraph on Pueblo rituals)

Discussed in Chapter: Two

Riley, P. (1998). *Food chains.* Danbury, CT: Franklin Watts.
Title: *Food Chains*
Author: Peter Riley
Informational Writing Tool: Using precise language and domain-specific vocabulary
Related Common Core Standards: W.4.2d, W.5.2d
Excerpt that Demonstrates Concept:

"Omnivores may search in many places for their food." (p. 10)

Discussed in Chapter: Six

Sattler, H. R. (1989). *The book of eagles.* New York, NY: Lothrop, Lee & Shepard Books.
Title: *The Book of Eagles*
Author: Helen Roney Sattler
Informational Writing Tool: Using precise language and domain-specific vocabulary

Related Common Core Standards: W.4.2d, W.5.2d
Excerpt that Demonstrates Concept:

"Others strap transmitters to the backs of fledglings and track them with satellites." (p. 30)

Discussed in Chapter: Six

Singer, M. (2007). *Venom*. Plain City, OH: Darby Creek Publishing.
Title: *Venom*
Author: Marilyn Singer
Informational Writing Tool: Using precise language and domain-specific vocabulary
Related Common Core Standards: W.4.2d, W.5.2d
Excerpt that Demonstrates Concept:

"The proteins in various toxins—often in the form of enzymes—attack cells and tissues, disrupt communication between nerve endings, and cause other damage." (p. 6)

Discussed in Chapter: Six

Another Informational Writing Tool in this Book: Crafting a concluding section
Related Common Core Standards: W.3.2d, W.4.2e, W.5.2e
Excerpt that Demonstrates Concept:

"Unfortunately, many of these [venomous] animals are in danger. They are losing their habitats or are being sickened by pollutants and waste. They are being sold as pets—or killed by pets. They are slaughtered by people for their skins, for souvenirs, or simply for no better reason than because folks just don't like them.

Unless we learn to appreciate these creatures, we won't safeguard them and their environments. If we don't safeguard them, we will never uncover or understand all of the marvels of venom and other biotoxins. We will lose the grace of a jellyfish, the trill of a toad, the beauty of a butterfly, the surprise of a snake, and even the awesome scariness of a big, hairy spider with its venomous fangs—and that would be a big loss indeed." (p. 89)

Discussed in Chapter: Seven

Silverstein, A., Silverstein, V., & Nunn, L. S. (1998). *Symbiosis*. Brookfield, CT: Twenty-First Century Books.
Title: *Symbiosis*
Authors: Alvin Silverstein, Virginia Silverstein, and Laura Silverstein Nunn
Informational Writing Tool: Adding features that aid comprehension
Related Common Core Standards: W.3.2a, W.4.2a, W.5.2a
Excerpts that Demonstrate Concept:

"Making Food Useful" (p.11), "Plants that Need Fixing" (p. 15), "Good Fungi" (p. 16) (Section headings)
"Green algae will grow on several of these giant clams, which will use the algae for food." (p. 37) (Photo caption)
"Ecology: Studies of symbiotic relationships and their interaction with the environment; genetic engineering to make positive relationships more effective and suppress parasites." (p. 53) ("Career Watch: Symbiosis" text box)

Discussed in Chapter: Three

Silverstein, A., Silverstein, V., & Nunn, L. S. (1998). *The grizzly bear*. Brookfield, CT: The Millbrook Press.
Title: *The Grizzly Bear*
Authors: Alvin Silverstein, Virginia Silverstein, and Laura Silverstein Nunn
Informational Writing Tool: Linking ideas
Related Common Core Standards: W.3.2c, W.4.2c, W.5.2c
Excerpt that Demonstrates Concept:

"When there is a small population of grizzlies, the mating pair will stay together for two to three weeks. However, in a larger population both the male and female may wander off and may have several different mating partners." (p. 27)

Discussed in Chapter: Five

Spilsbury, L., & Spilsbury, R. (2003). *Crushing avalanches*. Chicago, IL: Heinemann Library.
Title: *Crushing Avalanches*
Authors: Louise Spilsbury and Richard Spilsbury
Informational Writing Tool: Developing a topic

Related Common Core Standards: W.3.2b, W.4.2b, W.5.2b
Excerpt that Demonstrates Concept:

"When avalanches hit towns or cities, large numbers of people may face other dangers. The force of an avalanche can trap people under collapsed buildings or inside cars. It can pull down power lines that may electrocute people. Power lines can also make sparks that start fires." (p. 19)

Discussed in Chapter: Four

Snodgrass, M. E. (1991). *Air pollution.* Marco, FL: Bancroft-Sage.
Title: *Air Pollution*
Author: Mary Ellen Snodgrass
Informational Writing Tool: Adding features that aid comprehension
Related Common Core Standards: W.3.2a, W.4.2a, W.5.2a
Excerpts that Demonstrate Concept:

"Stopping Air Pollution at Home" (p. 31), "Making Our Nation a Better Neighbor" (p. 32), "Reducing Pollution from Cars" (p. 34), "Making Safer Factories" (p. 34) (Section headings in the chapter on "Cleaning the Air")
   "Generators from power plants can produce strong gases that escape through smokestacks, causing serious threats to clean air." (p. 21) (Photo caption)

Discussed in Chapter: Three

Stewart, M. (2001). *Reptiles.* New York, NY: Children's Press.
Title: *Reptiles*
Author: Melissa Stewart
Informational Writing Tool: Introducing a topic
Related Common Core Standards: W.3.2a, W.4.2a, W.5.2a
Excerpt that Demonstrates Concept:

"A snake flicks its long tongue as it slithers along the ground. A turtle sits on a rotting log and basks in the sun. A crocodile grabs a fish with its mighty jaws. These are the images that come to mind when someone says the word 'reptile.'" (p. 5)

Discussed in Chapter: One

Stille, D. R. (2004). *Cheetahs*. Minneapolis, MN: Compass Point Books.
Title: *Cheetahs*
Author: Darlene R. Stille
Informational Writing Tool: Grouping related information together
Related Common Core Standards: W.3.2a, W.4.2a, W.5.2a
Excerpts that Demonstrate Concept:

"The Cheetah's Body" (p. 6), "Where Cheetahs Live" (p. 12), "How Cheetahs Live" (p. 16) (Chapter titles in the book)
  "The cheetah's body is built for speed. It has long, thin legs that help it run fast. Its spine acts like a spring to help it leap forward. It has claws that act like spikes on running shoes to keep it from slipping. It also has a large heart and large blood vessels. These give its body the oxygen it needs to run fast." (p. 9) (Paragraph from the chapter titled "The Cheetah's Body)

Discussed in Chapter: Two

Todd, A. M. (2003). *Sitting Bull*. Mankato, MN: Blue Earth Books.
Title: *Sitting Bull*
Author: Anne M. Todd
Informational Writing Tool: Linking ideas
Related Common Core Standards: W.3.2c, W.4.2c, W.5.2c
Excerpt that Demonstrates Concept:

"Sitting Bull's parents named him Jumping Badger, but no one called him by that name. Instead, people called him Hunk-es-ni, which means slow." (p. 9)

Discussed in Chapter: Five

Wahl, G. (2014). World Cup preview 2014. *Sports Illustrated, 120* (23), 38–44.
Title: "Word Cup Preview 2014"
Author: Grant Wahl
Informational Writing Tool: Using precise language and domain-specific vocabulary
Related Common Core Standards: W.4.2d, W.5.2d
Excerpts that Demonstrate Concept:

"Corner kick" (p. 39), "hand ball" (p. 42)

Discussed in Chapter: Six

Woods, M., & Woods, M. B. (2007). *Tsunamis*. Minneapolis, MN: Lerner
Publications Company.
Title: *Tsunamis*
Authors: Michael Woods and Mary Woods
Informational Writing Tool: Developing a topic
Related Common Core Standards: W.3.2b, W.4.2b, W.5.2b
Excerpts that Demonstrate Concept:

"Tsunamis are waves that crash down onto shore and cause disasters. Disasters are events that cause great destruction. Some tsunamis are more than 100 feet (30 m) high. They would reach up
to the tenth-floor windows on a skyscraper. Tsunamis can be
hundreds of miles long. They can travel thousands of miles at
speeds of nearly 600 miles per hour (970 km/hr). That's as fast as
jet airplanes fly." (p. 6)
 "When the water pulled back after the 2004 Indian Ocean tsunami, it left a big mess. More than 500,000 people in southern Asia
and eastern Africa had broken bones, cuts, and other injuries. They
needed doctors and nurses. But the monster waves had smashed
hospitals and doctor's offices. Doctors and nurses also were dead
or hurt." (p. 36)

Discussed in Chapter: Four

Zimmerman, K. (2004). *Steam locomotives*. Honesdale, PA: Boyds Mills
Press.
Title: *Steam Locomotives*
Author: Karl Zimmerman
Informational Writing Tool: Linking ideas
Related Common Core Standards: W.3.2c, W.4.2c, W.5.2c
Excerpts that Demonstrate Concept:

"Though the locomotive was built in Britain, it was in the United
States that a warning bell and headlight were added. Also added
was a pilot or 'cowcatcher,' which was attached to the front of the
engine and designed to push obstructions, including cattle, off the
tracks." (p. 15)
 "The *Best Friend* was quite a success, hauling as many as five cars
with fifty passengers. Unfortunately, about five months after its
much-praised debut, the locomotive's fireman tied down its safety
valve because the hiss of escaping steam annoyed him." (p. 14)

Discussed in Chapter: Five

Appendix
Reproducible Charts and Forms You Can Use in Your Classroom

This appendix contains reproducible versions of key charts and forms featured in this book. It is designed to help you put the ideas in this book into action in your classroom!

Figure 1.2 How the Introduction to a Book Performs the Key Actions of an Introduction

Action Performed by Introduction	Section of a Book that Performs this Action
1. Engage the reader	
2. Introduce key content	

Figure 3.1 Adding Features to Informational Writing

Feature you will add to your informational text.	Description of the feature.
1.	
2.	

Figure 5.1 Linking Ideas Activity using Published Work

Title and author of the book you used	Example from text that contains language that links ideas	Example rewritten without language that links ideas	Why you think the language that links ideas is important to the original text

Figure 5.5 Linking Ideas Activity Using Student's Own Work

Text you created that uses language that links ideas	That text, without the language that links ideas	Why you think the language that links ideas is important to the original text you created

Figure 6.3 Specific Vocabulary in Published Text Analysis Chart

Title and author of the book you used	Line from text containing domain-specific vocabulary	Line from text with domain-specific vocabulary replaced by more general language	Why you think the domain-specific vocabulary is important to the original text

Figure 6.5 Analyzing Domain-Specific Vocabulary in Students' Own Work

Sentence you created that uses domain-specific vocabulary	That sentence, with the domain-specific vocabulary replaced by more general language	Why you think the domain-specific vocabulary is important to the original sentence you created

Figure 7.2 How a Published Book Performs the Key Actions of a Conclusion

Action Performed by Conclusion	Book you Used	Excerpt from the Book that Performs this Action
1 Highlight the significance of the piece's topic.		
2 Leave readers with a final thought or message about this topic.		

© 2015, *The Informational Writing Toolkit: Using Mentor Texts in Grades 3-5*, Sean Ruday, Taylor & Francis

Figure 8.1 Evaluation Criteria for Introducing a Topic

Writing Tool	Evaluation Criteria	Possible Points	Your Score
Introducing a topic	◆ Does the introduction engage the reader by grabbing his or her attention? ◆ Does the introduction introduce key content and information related to the topic of the piece?	4	

Comments:

Figure 8.2 Evaluation Criteria for Grouping Related Information Together

Writing Tool	Evaluation Criteria	Possible Points	Your Score
Grouping related information together	◆ Does the author use organizational elements such as chapters, sections, and paragraphs to group related information together? ◆ Is the information in these organizational elements clearly related?	4	

Comments:

Figure 8.3 Evaluation Criteria for Adding Features that Aid Comprehension

Writing Tool	Evaluation Criteria	Possible Points	Your Score
Adding features that aid comprehension	◆ Does the text includes features such as headings, photographs, illustrations, charts, and graphs? ◆ Are these features clearly related to the piece's topic? ◆ Do these features enhance the reader's understanding of the topic?	4	

Comments:

Figure 8.4 Evaluation Criteria for Developing a Topic

Writing Tool	Evaluation Criteria	Possible Points	Your Score
Developing a Topic	◆ Does the text include information such as facts, definitions, details, quotations, and examples? ◆ Are these pieces of information clearly related to the piece's topic? ◆ Does this information help the reader understand the topic?	4	

Comments:

Figure 8.5 Evaluation Criteria for Linking Ideas

Writing Tool	Evaluation Criteria	Possible Points	Your Score
Linking Ideas	◆ Does the text include words and phrases that link the ideas in the piece? ◆ Do these words and phrases clearly show the relationship between the linked ideas?	4	

Comments:

Figure 8.6 Evaluation Criteria for Using Precise Language and Domain-Specific Vocabulary

Writing Tool	Evaluation Criteria	Possible Points	Your Score
Using Precise Language and Domain-Specific Vocabulary	◆ Does the piece include precise language and domain-specific vocabulary when presenting information to the reader? ◆ Is it clear that the precise language and domain-specific vocabulary used relates to the author's message?	4	

Comments:

Figure 8.7 Evaluation Criteria for Crafting a Concluding Section

Writing Tool	Evaluation Criteria	Possible Points	Your Score
Crafting a Concluding Section	◆ Does the conclusion highlight the significance of the piece's topic? ◆ Does the conclusion leave readers with a final thought or message about the topic? ◆ Does the conclusion go beyond summarizing the paper's content?	4	

Comments:

CPSIA information can be obtained
at www.ICGtesting.com
Printed in the USA
FSOW04n2218221116
27743FS

9 781138 832060